There is no greater gift that can be [illegible] teaching someone to know and be [illegible] by God. In [illegible] *Still*, Brian Heasley is offering that gift. Brian is a man who sits at the feet of Jesus, and in these pages, you'll want to join him there.

TYLER STATON, national director of 24–7 Prayer USA

This book describes the direction I would like to go in my prayer life. The author reminds us that there is not one but many ways to pray and that we can listen to our own minds and hearts to discern which way is best for us at this time. Since I am well into my senior years, I especially appreciated his reminder that God surprises us with new things in every season of our lives. So true!

ALICE FRYLING, spiritual director and author of *Aging Faithfully: The Holy Invitation of Growing Older*

A practical and vitally important framework for enriching this daily discipline.

MARK SAYERS, author of *A Non-Anxious Presence: How a Changing and Complex World Will Create a Remnant of Renewed Christian Leaders*

Whether you are experienced in the daily habit of "quiet time" with God, starting out, or seeking refreshment, I wholeheartedly commend this beautiful book. A witty, vulnerable, utterly practical, rich, and creative guide, it will assist every genuine seeker after God.

THE RIGHT REVEREND SOPHIE JELLEY, Bishop of Doncaster

Brian Heasley

Be Still

A Simple Guide to Quiet Times

A NavPress resource published in alliance
with Tyndale House Publishers

NavPress is the publishing ministry of The Navigators, an international Christian organization and leader in personal spiritual development. NavPress is committed to helping people grow spiritually and enjoy lives of meaning and hope through personal and group resources that are biblically rooted, culturally relevant, and highly practical.

For more information, visit NavPress.com.

*I would like to dedicate this book to my father,
Billy Heasley, whose life of prayer, perseverance, and
discipline has been an inspiration to me.*

Romans 8:28

Contents

Foreword

Pete Greig, 24–7 Prayer

You will never change your life until you change something you do daily. The secret of your success is found in your daily routine.

JOHN MAXWELL

I BELIEVE THAT THIS BOOK is going to be enormously important in your life for two reasons: First, it is going to *inspire* you to cultivate a deeper daily encounter with God. Second, it's going to *equip* you simply and practically to do so. If John Maxwell is even half right and our ultimate destinies and identities are indeed determined by the details of our daily routines, nothing could possibly be more transformational than the ultimate holy habit of a daily quiet time. It really could be as important as that.

Brian Heasley and I are close friends. We traveled the world together and spent the best part of our adult lives serving the Lord side by side. We laughed a very great deal, argued, apologized, embarked on adventures, wept—and of course we prayed together. I recounted some of Brian's amazing story in a book called *Dirty Glory*, but here in this one he shares the real secret of his life, the key to his ministry, the heart and soul of his faith. Best of all, he teaches us how to do the same.

A few weeks ago I stayed in Brian's house and saw the chair, described in this book, that is his place of daily encounter with the Lord. He tends to wake earlier than I do, so I often come down in the morning, wherever we are in the world—on the Mediterranean island of Ibiza, high in the Rocky Mountains, even in Windsor Castle—to find Brian sitting quietly with his Bible and a cup of coffee, spending time alone with his Lord. Sometimes he will call me during the day from far away to inquire about some detail of my life, or to share something he has sensed from the Lord, and I know that it is because he has been praying for me that day. Occasionally I've asked him without warning to share a devotional thought at a staff meeting or at a leaders' retreat, and Brian always, without fail, has something insightful to say—drawn, no doubt, from his quiet time that morning.

Henri Nouwen, the Dutch priest who swapped professorships at Yale and Harvard for life within a community of mentally disabled adults, wrote:

> We have, indeed, to fashion our own desert
> where we can withdraw every day, shake off our
> compulsions, and dwell in the gentle healing
> presence of our Lord. Without such a desert we
> will lose our soul while preaching the gospel
> to others. But with such a spiritual abode, we
> will become increasingly conformed to him in
> whose Name we minister.[1]

Brian is someone who learned to "fashion [his] own desert," and it is in this space that he has conformed a little more each day into the likeness of Jesus. But one of the things I so appreciate about this book is that there's no hint of legalism or guilt. I found myself excited by Brian's example and equipped by his insights without any hint of a heavy *should*, just a tantalizing *could*.

But my excitement about the release of this book has been mingled with astonishment that it needed to be written in the first place. Talk to any of the great heroes of the faith (not just the famous ones, but the quiet, humble ones you may already know personally), and you will quickly discover that the key to their faith is the time they spend daily with the Lord in prayer and biblical reflection. Quiet times really are that fundamental to a real relationship with Jesus. And yet the research reveals that, tragically, this cardinal practice is declining, especially among the young, even at a time when the Bible is more freely accessible than ever before.

Something within me rises up and says, "Not on our watch! We can't let the quiet time die! We are called to make disciples of Jesus. Not just church attenders who can sing songs and say the creeds without their fingers crossed but a generation who truly knows how to walk and talk with the Lord intimately and how to be shaped by his Word daily."

Bewilderingly, while there are plenty of devotional materials available, there are very few resources that actually, and practically, teach new Christians (and those who've been around the block a few times) how to go about having a quiet time. Perhaps, most charitably, this is because a quiet time is such a private thing that leaders shy away from letting others into their intimate space with the Lord? Whatever the reason, I am so delighted that Brian was willing to open his heart to us, drawing together his own hard-won insights gleaned over decades of daily quiet times, and teaching them to us so powerfully and practically in this book.

So yes, I believe that this could be one of the most important books you will read this year. My heartfelt prayer is that it will help you, amid life's many distractions and distortions, to fashion your own desert, cultivating the delightful discipline of pausing daily simply to Be Still.

Pete Greig
24–7 Prayer International and Emmaus Rd church

Introduction

OVER THE YEARS I'VE LEARNED that my relationship with Jesus is less about trying harder or climbing higher and more a process of being invited deeper. I've been a Christian since I was five years old, and I've recently turned fifty. That's forty-five years of journeying through the seasons with Jesus into the greatest adventure I've ever known. I've discovered along the way that most of our lives are unrehearsed, seldom as neat or linear as we would like them to be.

My life started well in Belfast, Northern Ireland. I come from a great family with parents who were both dedicated to serving God. This dedication took them to England to lead a small church in Essex, when I was eight years old. Sadly, my mother passed away from ovarian cancer when I was eleven, and this became a defining and painful moment for our family. My faith took a battering, and as I battled through grief I also battled through my relationship with God.

For many years I used to think I was in some sort of battle between faith and doubt, but I've come to realize that it wasn't a battle at all; I had faith and I had doubt. I had to learn to live with both, but I got to choose which one to feed and cultivate.

For a long time, I didn't feed my faith, which in turn meant I didn't have deep roots. This led to a certain dissatisfaction with life, where doubt flourished like an untamed weed, and I began to struggle to truly function as a Christian. I lived with this dualism throughout the entirety of my teenage years, wrestling with who I wanted to be, who I imagined others wanted me to be, and my own understanding of who God wanted me to be. I experienced incredible swings and roundabouts in my spiritual life. I could go from responding to an altar call in a meeting on a Sunday morning to smoking a huge joint on my way to work on a Monday. I could help energetically at the midweek children's group in church and on my way home throw that same energy into a street fight. I could sing sweet songs to Jesus, and then let my imagination run riot with all sorts of wild fantasies and lustful thoughts. I could give, but I wanted to get. I could feel love, but I sometimes showed hate. I was full of contradiction and conflict, but I knew how to perform differently in the different settings I was in, and I honestly thought I was getting away with living my double life.

Then it got too hard to maintain. When I was seventeen, the wheels came off all the lives I was trying to live. My choices became erratic and very soon led to me being asked to leave college—and home. By eighteen, I was homeless, jobless, and seemingly out of options. I rapidly lost confidence, becoming introverted and withdrawn, which probably wasn't helped by all the weed I was smoking. I had no plan, no obvious future; I became indifferent to myself and my life, taking a step back and letting life happen to me instead of initiating any form of proactivity that would bring change. I had an inner God awareness, directing my thoughts to him, but not one that affected my external behavior. But as I muddled into my twenties, all that was about to change.

After a few visits to prison, life caught up with me, and so did God. I made a conscious choice that I would give the rest of my life to him. That was nearly thirty years ago; I am now by no means perfect, but I have been a husband for twenty-nine years, raised two children to adulthood, and enjoyed a full life serving God.

Prayer had always been a part of my childhood, from the little picture that hung on our bedroom wall of a child kneeling with the simple words *Prayer changes things* to watching my father consistently get up early to pray. But since the moment I committed my life to God, prayer has remained at the forefront of my faith. I fully believe that prayer— a devotion to relationship, encounter, and conversation with God—is the root of all we do. It's the presence of the Holy Spirit, the ministry of Jesus, and time spent with the Father that make us who we are. Directionless lives are given meaning in our relationship with God; this relationship is grown in community, through discipleship, and by establishing and developing our personal devotional lives.

One of the key ways I have sought to establish a rhythm

of prayer that sustains me through the various seasons of life is through a *quiet time*. A quiet time is simply a daily time that I set aside to specifically tune in to God through prayer, Bible reading, and reflection. It's a time when I not only speak to God but also ask God to speak to me. It also gives me the opportunity to examine my life on a daily basis, to see if I am truly practicing my faith. It is the wellspring, oasis, and source of my life as a Christian.

For me this requires the first hour of my day, a chair, a Bible, a journal, and a strong cup of coffee; but, as we'll see in this book, quiet times don't have to look a certain way. At 24–7 Prayer, we have been helping create spaces for quiet times for years, and often not in the quietest of places! Ever since we started in 1999, we have encouraged groups of people to set up and pray in "prayer spaces" for twenty-four hours, seven days a week, and these spaces are now in place in church buildings and town halls and empty main street shops, on battleships, in breweries, in prisons, in schools, and in homes and palaces across two-thirds of the nations in the world. These tend to be creative spaces full of fairy lights and places to sit and write and respond, but they really only create one thing: an opportunity to spend time with God.

Prayer in these spaces is more than just closing your eyes; these are places where you can paint, write, sing, and become involved with activities that help you engage with God. Even though they look different all over the world, they are intentional spaces for spending time with God.

The Bible tells us that Jesus actively sought out times and

places to pray; he went to the desert, to the mountain, to the garden, to the Temple. His prayer life had intentionality, and that intentionality was fueled by the desire to spend time with his Father. The Bible says, "Be still and wait patiently for the LORD" (Psalm 37:7, NIrV), which may be why the concept of a regular quiet time feels so foreign to some of us. Many of us aren't particularly good at practicing stillness or patience—I get frustrated if a page loads slowly on my laptop! We live in a busy and very immediate culture, yet this verse calls us to be still and to wait patiently. It is not meant as an onerous obligation but an invitation from God to enter a place of encounter with him.

Some Franciscan monks once described Psalm 46:10, "Be still, and know that I am God," as the gateway to prayer, and yet, for me personally, I once felt like God said to me, *Brian, you are not very still, and you often try to be God!* Maybe, like me, you need to reimagine quiet times as a gateway into a place of stillness, where we can know the omnipotent, omniscient, omnipresent, immutable, eternal being who is God.

This gateway isn't static. I believe that we can live a life in which we know and feel God's presence at any time and in any place. In this transient age we need a portable faith. I want that sense of God's presence whether I'm at home, in the office, at the gym, out for a walk, with friends, at a party, or in the pub—wherever I am. And I'm convinced that the discipline of a quiet time is key to making this happen. Over the years I have developed a devotional routine— which means that every morning I spend time in the same chair—but I have learned that the devotion I have cultivated there, and the presence of God I've felt, must remain with me throughout the day, wherever I am. The quiet time strengthens my faith so that it is not shaken by geography, social-media likes, relational tension, or any of life's other variables.

I'm well aware that life isn't always easy and that we regularly experience challenges, big and small; however, in the midst of this, we can develop a deep spirituality that means we are not shaken and don't become broken as we remain deeply connected to God.

Every life is different, and as you read this book, one of the most liberating things you need to know is that everybody's prayer life is unique too. Our prayer lives will look different at different stages of life. In these pages are just a few simple ideas, some questions to ask yourself, and different points to reflect on—things that, over the last thirty or so years, I have found helpful. I hope they will help you to intentionally create and develop your own quiet time. They are not intended to be exhaustive, so do check out the bibliography at the end for more extensive books that will help you go deeper in each of these subjects. What I share in this book is not meant to be patronizing; whether you're new to this or have been practicing quiet times for decades, I hope that this book will be a tool that will help you develop and grow a quiet time that sustains you wherever you are and whatever you are going through.

1

Encounter

EVERY MORNING, I get up; make myself a cup of coffee; gather my journal, my Bible, and my books; and sit in the same chair in the corner of my living room. For the first hour of most mornings, I settle down in this spot and encounter God. A number of years ago, I wrote the following in my journal:

> Lord, I want to cultivate and remember the moment I
> have with you in this chair so that I can go there in my
> mind wherever I am. I need to be able to sink into the
> memory of the chair at any point. I have to maintain
> enough God awareness throughout the day to sink back

*into you at any given moment, to lean into you. My
time in the chair gives me muscle memory for the day.
I felt it somewhere random the other day, this familiar
morning feeling. . . . I chose to feel it, to become aware
of your presence in that particular moment.*

The encounter I have with God in my chair creates in me an awareness of God that lingers throughout the day. So let me ask you: Where is your chair?

The word *encounter* means "to meet with someone," "to contend with someone," or "to come across." For instance, we say things like "I'm encountering problems at work" or read classic books that say things like "We will encounter the enemy at dawn." We also have encounters with people; I have had some quirky meetings over the years that haven't gone well, which I have left thinking, *That was an interesting encounter!*

When I first encountered my wife, I was new to our church and just out of prison. I would arrive with enthusiasm most Sundays, and Tracy would be playing saxophone in the church worship band. (We should bring saxophone back to worship. I would love to hear a few Bruce Springsteen-esque sax solos on a Sunday.) I would sincerely embrace the worship but be distracted enough to put on my best worship face, all the time maneuvering into a position where I might also be able to catch Tracy's eye. For a few weeks I thought this strategy was proving successful. I felt the chemistry, I could see the curiosity—the excitement in her eyes—as she gazed back at me. Eventually I plucked up the courage to ask her out on a date, and, before long, we were married.

While dating, I discovered that my future wife was short-sighted; she could not see beyond the end of the stage she was standing on! She had not once looked at me; I had completely misread this moment. But still, it was an encounter that changed me.

Encounters Change Us

We all encounter people who have a profound impact on our lives: spouses, children, teachers, parents, friends, grandparents, pastors, and leaders; encounters with these people change us. Situations that we encounter, good and bad, also have a profound effect on us—illness, a near-death moment, unemployment, conflict, tragedy, a new job, the birth of a child, travel, discovering new things.

My first encounter with God definitely changed me. If you're reading this as a Christian today, I'm guessing it is because at some point you encountered God and came to the realization that he was real and that he had sent his Son, Jesus, to die for you. You encountered him and received your salvation. My hope is that this was more than a one-off encounter.

Although I encountered God in the moment of salvation, it became clear to me that I would need to have regular encounters with him if I was going to sustain my Christian faith. The reason I go to my chair in the morning is because I desire regular encounters with him.

Encounter Began in a Garden

The first regular encounter that we read of in the Bible is that of God walking with Adam and Eve "in the cool of the day" (Genesis 3:8). Sadly, we learn of this encounter when it is on the verge of breakdown:

> Then the man and his wife heard the sound of the LORD God as he was walking in the garden in the cool of the day, and they hid from the LORD God among the trees of the garden. But the LORD God called to the man, "Where are you?"
>
> GENESIS 3:8-9

Ellicott's *Bible Commentary for English Readers* says:

> Jehovah appears here as the owner of the Paradise, and as taking in it His daily exercise; for the verb is in the reflexive conjugation, and means "walking for pleasure." The time is "the cool (literally, *the wind*) of the day," the hour in a hot climate when the evening breeze sets in, and men, rising from their noontide slumber, go forth for labour or recreation. In this description the primary lesson is that hitherto man had lived in close communication with God.[1]

Despite the slightly antiquated language of this commentary, the primary lesson we learn from this Bible passage is that humankind originally lived in close communication with

God. What a beautiful picture: God, as the owner of this paradise, took a walk for pleasure with Adam and Eve—with the implication that this was a regular occurrence, not a one-off! When I read that they "heard the sound of the LORD God," I believe they sensed his approach, heard the sound of his footsteps. I can almost picture them stopping, waiting, and listening, maybe with excitement rising, stilling themselves, getting ready to walk with God.

This is a striking depiction of God's original intent: rested people walking with the Creator-God, talking as friends. People regularly encountering God, people living in close communion with God. Then one day God's walking companions are nowhere in sight; they are hiding, and God calls out, "Where are you?" Something in me loves the weight of the old language of the King James Version, which has God calling, "Where art thou?" I think God still calls out regularly to his people, to you and me: "Where art thou?" And yet, does it seem likely that when God called out "Where are you?" to Adam and Eve he truly didn't know where they were, that somehow the all-knowing God had lost them?

Fear and shame about what they had done wrong had caused them to hide, and it can do the same thing to us. This thought comes: *If I'm alone with God, he's going to see things in me that I don't want him to; I am going to be confronted with my lack of knowledge, my sin, my weakness.* I'm frightened that I will be found out as shallow and weak and useless at living this whole Christian life. Maybe I will skip the personal encounter and just get busy doing things—good things, church things, Christian things. I will go to church meetings and encounter God in a crowd, but please, not on my own. He's going to gaze into my soul and find it shallow, dark, hypocritical, and weak. The shame hinders me from encountering God deeply. Some commentators say that God was not calling out to find out Adam and Eve's physical location—rather, what condition they were in: As we might say today, "Where are you at?" Sometimes I'd rather not answer that question!

God pursues us. It is a gracious pursuit, one that is laced with kindness, in order for him to help us recover and restore. We do not need to fear encounter because in genuine encounter we are made whole. Christ's intervention through his sacrificial death nullified the separation we experience because of sin and death. Amazing reassurance is given in Romans 8:1-2: "Therefore, there is now no condemnation for those who are in Christ Jesus, because through Christ Jesus the law of the Spirit who gives life has set you free from the law of sin and death." The original plan is reset: God walking and talking with people without barriers.

Where's Your Garden?

The Hebrew word for "garden" is *gannah*, which literally means "a covered or hidden place." Gardens in biblical settings were usually small, walled enclosures, tranquil spaces in which you could tuck yourself out of sight and find a moment of rest. You can find many examples of these in

Morocco, Tunisia, or even Seville in Spain. These small gardens aimed to replicate the feel of larger gardens, in which you might find winding paths, running water, aromatic shade trees and plants, beautiful places to sit, fountains trickling and bubbling, and birds singing. Both settings would be beautiful places to relax and be refreshed in a hot, dry country. We don't know exactly what the garden in which Adam and Eve walked with God looked like, how tame or wild it felt, but it seems likely that in a time when God's creation was new and unspoiled, it would have been an inviting and refreshing place.

The chair where I spend my quiet times is my metaphorical "garden," my place of encounter, and morning is my time. I wake early and, at this stage of life, feeding and organizing small children for the day is no longer part of my morning routine. Location and time of day can be completely different for everyone. Your "garden" could be your car, your gym, out in the open air, or even in your bed. (Some of those may take a little more effort to turn into a quiet space, but it can be done.) Taking time in the morning is a great way to start the day, but it may be that a less distracted time for you is a walk during your lunch break—or perhaps you feel more able to focus at the end of the busyness of whatever your regular day holds. What's important is that you find a location and time for encounter within each day. I regularly travel for work, and while I am away, my encounter time changes and the location changes. But whatever my schedule looks like, I have learned to identify the time within each day for a quiet time. In every season it's possible to find something that works.

For Jesus, the flow of his life and ministry was prayerful, reflective, and overflowed from regular encounters with his Father, and we would do well to learn from him.

Encounter When Life Is Good

When things were going well, Jesus prayed. Early on in his Gospel, Mark writes about Jesus healing many who were sick. Word spread quickly—so quickly that while Jesus was staying in the home of the mother-in-law of his disciple Peter, "the whole town gathered at the door" hoping to meet him (Mark 1:33). Many more healings followed, with people continuing to come from all over town. This was early on in the ministry of Jesus, and it already looked very successful. Thinking back to my own time as a church leader, this would have been my dream, the whole town turning up at the door, seeking an encounter with Jesus. This would be classed as real breakthrough—things would be going well, and other church leaders would probably visit to see what God was doing so they could have the same experience in their own towns.

But then we read, "Very early in the morning, while it was still dark, Jesus got up, left the house and went off to a solitary place, where he prayed" (Mark 1:35). In the midst of success and breakthrough, receptive crowds, people keen to become followers and eager to hear his words and witness his actions, Jesus took himself away from all of it and removed himself to a solitary place for a quiet time. We don't know what he did in this quiet time, but Mark chooses to mention it, so it seems that there is something he wants the reader to understand.

The disciples came looking for him, perhaps rather bemused by his disappearance, and upon finding him, exclaimed, "Everyone is looking for you!" (Mark 1:37). They were basically saying, "Let's get back to it. Let's build on this breakthrough, seize this moment, ride this wave!" It's clear that God was dramatically at work in this time; this wasn't something that the disciples were used to experiencing. They could have created a revival center; people would have traveled from near and far to join them; from there, Jesus could have established his rule and reign. Job done, mission accomplished.

Jesus didn't go back to where the crowds were waiting; instead, he announced, "Let us go somewhere else—to the nearby villages—so I can preach there also. That is why I have come" (Mark 1:38). We don't read whether the disciples were more confused or excited by this unexpected move; all we know is that Jesus came out of a place of prayer determined to preach in other places. I once heard a wise preacher speak of two things that will slow us down in our Christian walk: One is a wrong sense of responsibility; the other is responding to the wrong opportunities. I think that when we visit the garden, the quiet place, we are reminded of who we are and that God is in control.

I have observed that people are more likely to stop meeting

with God when life is good than they are when life is tough. Encounter can disappear from our lives when success leads us away from prioritizing a quiet time. It's easy for the adrenaline, the crowds, the acclaim, the status, or the money to subtly divert our attention away from God, the source of our life and peace. All these were on offer to Jesus at this point in his ministry, but that is not what he chose. He chose to withdraw to the quiet place. He chose to ignore the allure of success and distraction of attention and continue the journey he knew he was called to. He didn't imply that success was in and of itself wrong; it was more that he didn't allow the good that is found in success to lead him away from his quiet times.

Similarly, in the Old Testament, when the children of Israel had traveled for many years through the inhospitable desert environment and were finally on the cusp of entering a life of rest and prosperity, God cautioned them through the voice of Moses: "When you eat and are satisfied, be careful that you do not forget the LORD, who brought you out of Egypt, out of the land of slavery" (Deuteronomy 6:11-12). When we are full and content, confident in our self-sufficiency, we can forget to go to our chair and be nourished by the Lord. Instead, we need to cultivate a holy determination to go to the quiet place of encounter in success.

Encounter When Life Is Busy

As we move further into the Gospel of Mark, we read of Jesus being very busy:

Then, because so many people were coming and going that they did not even have a chance to eat, he said to them, "Come with me by yourselves to a quiet place and get some rest."

So they went away by themselves in a boat to a solitary place. But many who saw them leaving recognized them and ran on foot from all the towns and got there ahead of them. When Jesus landed and saw a large crowd, he had compassion on them, because they were like sheep without a shepherd. So he began teaching them many things.

MARK 6:31-34

It's clear that Jesus and his disciples were under a huge amount of pressure with great demands being made on their time, so much so that they didn't have enough time to stop and eat properly. When we neglect our basic physical needs, it's often the case that we are also neglecting our spiritual needs. Jesus said to his disciples, "Come with me by yourselves to a quiet place." They jumped in a boat and headed for a solitary place to escape the crowd, but the crowd followed them. Life is like this; the crowd follows us. Sometimes our solitary place becomes crowded: crowded by the busyness of life itself, as well as by the distractions, worries, and preoccupations that come with it. Like the crowd, these things can either prevent us from entering the quiet place or follow us into our quiet place, disrupting our well-intentioned plans.

Jesus' response to the crowd and everything that they brought with them was one of compassion. He attended to them before dismissing them: "Jesus made his disciples get into the boat and go on ahead of him to Bethsaida, while he dismissed the crowd. After leaving them, he went up on a mountainside to pray" (Mark 6:45-46).

Becoming still in the solitary place during a time of busyness can sometimes take more effort than usual. It sounds strange to say that we have to work harder at becoming still—but in practice, it can feel like that. Like climbing a mountain, we push harder and climb higher to reach the mountaintop and find a breakthrough. I've climbed mountains—though not many, if I'm completely honest—and it's not easy. It takes time and energy. But reaching a summit offers fresh perspective and a different view of the world. We don't know what happened when Jesus dismissed the crowd and went up that mountain, but we do know that after he came down, he walked on water!

One of the hardest things to do when I'm at my busiest is to take longer than usual with my quiet time. With so much ahead that needs my attention, the temptation is to rush in and out again. But I've learned that my quiet time is more important than ever when there's a lot in my schedule or on my mind. In my quiet time, I find that the Lord comes and resources me with a fresh perspective and renewed energy.

Encounter When in Crisis

For me, gardens in the Bible represents intimacy: First, the intimacy that Adam and Eve experienced in the beginning as they walked and talked with God; later, the intimate encounter of Jesus with his Father in another garden. This account gives us insight into Jesus' time of greatest turmoil and distress but also his ultimate submission and obedience to his Father. Knowing that torture, the cross, and death were imminent, Jesus said to his disciples, "My soul is overwhelmed with sorrow to the point of death" (Mark 14:34). Then, going a little farther, he fell to the ground and prayed that if possible, the hour might pass from him. "*Abba*, Father," he said, "everything is possible for you. Take this cup from me. Yet not what I will, but what you will" (Mark 14:36).

What a powerful moment of intimacy in a time of unimaginable crisis. Before the action came prayer; before the redemptive act that would offer salvation to all humankind, a moment of absolute intimacy took place in a garden. What was lost in a garden was restored in a garden. In the Garden of Eden, Adam surrendered to his own will; in the garden of Gethsemane, Jesus surrendered to his Father's will.

Crisis brings out all sorts of responses in us. We turn to other people, and we do what we can to fix things—neither of these is wrong. But when we turn to God in a time of crisis, we receive strength to face the night as well as the day. We find hope in the midst of despair, comfort in the midst of sorrow, and perhaps deeper intimacy than at any other moment, where we find ourselves like children crying, "Father!" As someone who has experienced loss and grief, I know that these few lines inadequately cover the suffering that accompanies crisis, that it is a deep need that raises many questions. For this I would strongly recommend the book *God on Mute*, written by my dear friend Pete Greig.

Summary
When life is good, when life is busy, in a time of crisis, we observe Jesus prioritizing a quiet time. These were not some dull, Earl Grey–sipping, devotional musings of some distant monastic, ethereal contemplator. These were life-changing quiet times that led to miracles, transformation, revelation, and salvation—destiny-shaping quiet times.

Here are some things to think about as we come to the end of this chapter:

- Where are you? Where are you at?

- Where is your chair? Where is your garden?

- When is the best time for you to go there?

- Do you need to change the time or place of your encounter with God?

If you're finding the questions above difficult to answer, consider the following:

- Find a place: your car, your gym, your bedroom, a prayer room, a local church sanctuary, your prison cell, your armchair.

- Find a time: morning, evening, afternoon, whatever works best for you.

- Flexibility will set you free: Different circumstances and different seasons require different approaches for your encounters. But challenge yourself to start where you are. Whether you are in a season of success, busyness, or despair, God will meet you there.

2

Distraction

I'VE CRASHED THREE CARS, and each time it happened, I was distracted. Once I was admiring the reflection of my car in a large shop window, which meant that I failed to notice that the car in front of me had stopped. The next time, I was talking to my baby son in his car seat and failed to see that the traffic lights had turned red. The final collision happened as I approached a roundabout. I proceeded without first checking that the driver in front had also moved forward, the driver this time being my pregnant wife in her sister's car, which we had borrowed to pick up the new car I was driving and had owned for one hour. I'm guessing that if I offered you a lift, you would be nervous!

The *Cambridge Dictionary* describes distraction as "something that prevents someone from giving their attention to something else."[1] When it comes to prayer, Jesus knew that we could be distracted. He understood that if we are going to have a quiet time with God, we will have to be intentional about a few things.

Matthew 6:6 tells us that Jesus said, "When you pray, go into your room, close the door and pray to your Father, who is unseen. Then your Father, who sees what is done in secret, will reward you." With these simple words he gives us some advice on how we can pursue a quiet time. The word *room* used in this text originates from the Greek word *tameion*, which translates as "storeroom." The word is used several times throughout the Bible, mainly with a sense of a secret place or a secret hiding place. Bible scholar R. T. France elaborates: "This was an inner room, secluded, probably windowless, and possibly with the only lockable door in the house; it is thus proverbial for a secret place."[2]

Jesus was not saying that there is no place for public or communal prayer, and he was not forbidding us from praying with others. He was guiding us to a deeper place of personal prayer that will go on to enhance our public and communal prayer. To find a "probably windowless" room doesn't necessarily sound appealing or comfortable, but I don't think that's literally what is being recommended; it's more an encouragement to find a room that is absent of distraction where we can more fully focus on the Lord.

If we are to follow Jesus' instruction well, we need to be

intentional about a few things: our choice of location, our action, and our interaction.

- Jesus tells us, "When you pray, go . . ." *Go* is a simple word that implies intent; it's a command to position oneself somewhere else; in this case, go into your room, seek out an *intentional location*.

- Next we are told to "close the door." Again there is intent; not just moving into a different space but making the physical effort to close the door, to take *intentional action*.

- Then you pray. Having gone to a specific place and taken action to remove distraction, you can give attention to "pray to your Father," an *intentional interaction*.

A Windowless Room

In 1851, Danish philosopher Søren Kierkegaard wrote about creating silence.[3] I like that he didn't say to *find* silence, he said to *create* silence. For us to create an undistracted, windowless silence where we can be fully focused and present, a degree of intentionality is required.

It's hard to find a physically windowless room—in my house that would mean a closet. But it's not necessarily glass windows that are the problem. We have many other windows to distract us; most of them exist on our devices. We have windows into the world of news, windows into the world of social media, windows to shopping, windows to information, and windows to entertainment. Yet Jesus asks us to go into a secluded, windowless room to pray. This was in part a reaction to some of the pharisaic practices of his day, where some wanted their piety in prayer to be very visible to others; at the same time it was a plea for us to spend time quietly in seclusion with God in "the secret place" that R. T. France described.

We live in a time of information overload, where shutting ourselves away in a quiet, secluded spot free from distraction is a challenge to do every day. Still, it can and should be rewarding. In Jesus' words: "Then your Father, who sees what is done in secret, will reward you." There are rewards to be found in seclusion, and benefits to gain in the secret place of prayer.

As I have grown in my practice of quiet times, my Father has rewarded me for my pursuit of him. Let's be clear, this reward isn't physical or material; the most significant rewards I have received from pursuing a quiet time have been internal rewards. I have found peace, I have found joy, I have found contentment, I have found myself, and I have found God as I have pursued this practice. To be still, I need to be undistracted.

Before this sounds like a rant against technology, I think it is useful to understand that really the biggest hindrance to getting into a room, locking the door, and praying to my unseen Father lies in my mind, not in my device! It goes something like this:

It's Monday morning. I'm preparing for the week ahead. I settle down in my chair for a quiet time in my "secret place" and turn to my Bible to begin. I prayerfully approach the book of Romans, pondering the beauty of chapter 12—the sweep of the narrative, Paul's exhortation to offer ourselves as living sacrifices, the blueprint for the Christian way of life. The journey through chapters 12 through 15 is immense. I'm excited to be digging into this awe-inspiring section of Scripture, exploring the age-old question *How then should we live?*

I consider Paul's longing to journey to Rome; as a citizen by birth of the powerful Roman Empire, he yearned to see this great capital and the church that had become established there. I envisage what Rome might have been like in the first century AD, and soon my thoughts drift:

I have never been to Rome. I'd love to go, maybe for a cheap city break. I love Italy. I love Italian food. That reminds me, I saw some pasta in the fridge; maybe we should have that for supper. Wouldn't it be lovely with some shrimp? Perhaps I will pop to the supermarket later and pick some up. The last time I was there, there was a special offer on strawberries. Mmm, strawberries: We had this delightful strawberry dessert at my mother-in-law's last week. Oh my goodness, she asked to borrow my pressure washer. I must drop it off later. Maybe I should buy them their own pressure washer? I bet I can find one on eBay.

Boom! I've picked up my phone and am searching eBay for mid-priced pressure washers to give as a Christmas present to my in-laws, and it's only the middle of March. I have well and truly left my inner room and am vacantly staring outside at a world of online shopping, when I had set out to pray to my unseen Father!

Admittedly, this kind of meandering is not restricted to quiet times; it can happen during any meeting. We respond to the noise in our heads and merrily follow its winding path down a bunny trail. Perhaps it's boredom; maybe we are overstimulated; it could be due to tiredness, stress, or just too much coffee! Inside our heads, we can live a distracted life where outwardly we appear present but inwardly we are meandering!

What I'm talking about here is unfocused wandering, not the curious and constructive exploration of a new idea or thought. Eric Klinger explains the psychology of daydreaming: "Daydreaming—if you include mindwandering and reverie—turns out to be one of the central features of human life. It is rooted in processes essential to our survival, and it is connected in one way or another to virtually everything about us."[4] But as well as being one of the central features of human life, daydreaming has the power to sidetrack most of us from our inner room during a quiet time. It has the potential to lead us away from the very focus that gives us life. So we must learn to regulate our mindwandering.

I find it fascinating that we can wander out of our inner rooms entirely in our minds! When I consider the added distractions that surround us, I am amazed that anybody can focus. There is currently a lot of teaching about reclaiming the Sabbath, putting our phones away, slowing down our digital input—all of which is helpful and beneficial—but we can't power down our minds. We become distracted, even without the technological clutter of twenty-first-century life that has been created to help (distract) us! But if we solely blame technology for our distraction, we perhaps excuse ourselves too easily. In a time before the internet, C. S. Lewis wrote:

> We are always falling in love or quarrelling,
> looking for jobs or fearing to lose them, getting
> ill and recovering, following public affairs. If we
> let ourselves, we shall always be waiting for some
> distraction or other to end before we can really get
> down to our work. The only people who achieve
> much are those who want knowledge so badly
> that they seek it while the conditions are still
> unfavourable. Favourable conditions never come.[5]

Distractions will always be around us; if we wait for the moment where they cease to exist, we wait in vain. A new home, a different job, a change of church, new relationships, or any other external change will not remove distraction. Distraction may change, but it is never gone. When it comes to distraction, "favourable conditions never come." Instead, we must learn to find peace and focus despite distractions.

We must learn to deal with some of the internal distraction that is an obstacle to a quiet time.

The workday ahead, a film you watched, a conversation you need to have, what you will be eating for dinner: Most of the time, we can hold distractions in the background to pursue the focus that a quiet time requires. Occasionally one will push to the fore. Others will leap out and hijack your thoughts, seemingly from nowhere. Still others, like my Romans story, will be started by triggers! I have discovered a technique that can help with most of these distractions. It's just two simple steps—name your distraction and tame your distraction.

Name Your Distraction

Defining what is distracting you is really important; to define it, I find it helpful to name it. We constantly have background noise playing in our minds; it's like a running commentary that is observing and latching on to instant stimuli, triggering memories of past situations and events, and prompting thoughts about future events. A friend of mine calls this "head noise"—he would say you can't make it go away, but you can dial it down.

To dial it down, you need to know what it is—you need to identify it. Then you can name the distraction. Some days it's easier to name the distraction than others. I've found that when I can't quite put my finger on what the distraction is, it's worth stopping for a moment to try to identify it. I can normally name it within a few minutes!

In simple terms, it looks like this:

- *Become aware of your distraction.* Acknowledge that you are not as attentive as you would like to be.

- *Identify your distraction.* Take the extra few moments, if necessary, to work out exactly what it is that is distracting you.

- *Declare the name of your distraction.* Say to yourself, out loud, on paper, or internally, "I'm being distracted by . . ."

Having named your distraction, you can go on to the next step.

Tame Your Distraction

In taming your distraction, you think about the level of action required for the distraction you have named.

- *Respond to a distraction.* Some distractions require a response. If you keep thinking about a friend whose marriage is going through a tough time, this is a distraction that should lead to prayer.

- *Feed a distraction.* Give it what it wants, and it will go away quickly. If you find that you're consistently distracted by a rumbling tummy, this is a distraction that a couple of slices of toast or a bowl of oatmeal would sort out!

- *Delay a distraction.* If the distraction is a task that you need to remember to complete later in the day, it often helps to write it down and pick it up after your quiet time. If your phone keeps buzzing, switch it off.

- *Dismiss a distraction.* Sometimes it's just nonsense and needs to be ignored! Laugh at it, trash it, or burn it!

This is actually a really quick and simple process; it won't take long and will leave you free to move into the rest of your quiet time in a more focused way. I've also found that there are some physical actions that help to prevent distraction. It seems quite natural to engage our sight and hearing when we think about a quiet time. Engaging the sense of touch is also a good way to stop a distraction.

Practice the Tactile

Several years ago, a small team from 24–7 Prayer was asked to set up and host a prayer space in St. Paul's Cathedral in London. This is such a beautiful building, and perhaps one of the most impressive we could have found, in which to create a place for anybody to drop in and pray imaginatively and reflectively. We set up seven stations that facilitated a journey of prayer. At one of the stations were pieces of string; people were invited to tie five knots into a piece of string and then take it away as a reminder to pray for five friends who didn't yet know Jesus.

After a couple of days there, we heard that the then bishop of London would be visiting, and I was asked to show him around and explain the prayer stations to him. I greatly admire the now retired Right Reverend Richard Chartres, but he is slightly intimidating! He officiated at the royal wedding of Prince William and Kate Middleton and had the honor of preaching to the most people anyone ever has at any one time, as one billion people looked on from around the world. His role, his imposing height, and his booming voice, together with the awareness that St. Paul's was his stomping ground, made me very nervous.

As I showed him the prayer station with the pieces of string, the bishop turned to me and said, "These remind me of a Russian *chotki*. Do you have one?"

I was baffled and said, "No."

He replied, "Well then, you can have mine. I'll pop home and get it for you."

And with that, the bishop promptly walked out of St. Paul's Cathedral back to his house across the road, leaving behind a slightly bemused cluster of dignitaries. He returned quickly with this strange prayer rope made of one hundred knots, which were separated by a wooden bead every tenth knot. The bishop took a moment, looked me in the eye, and said, "I want to give you this *chotki* as a sign of gratitude for the work of 24–7 Prayer and all that you have done in inspiring prayer over the years." It was an extraordinary moment.

As he presented the *chotki* to me, he said, "This was made for me by a Siberian monk called Father Mercury." At this point my nerves got the better of me as, without really engaging my brain, I quipped, "Any relation to Freddie?" No one laughed. I swallowed my embarrassment, thanked him profusely for his incredibly kind gesture, and we moved on.

Anyway, I'm getting off topic—see how easy it is to get distracted? *Chotkis* are prayer ropes that originate from the Eastern Catholic and Eastern Orthodox traditions, generally used by monks to help count how many times they have prayed the Jesus Prayer: *Jesus Christ, Son of God, have mercy on me, a sinner.* In the traditional method, you pray the Jesus Prayer on every knot, and then on the tenth wooden bead you say the Lord's Prayer. I sometimes follow this pattern, but at other times I mix it up, praying for friends, or repeating other Bible phrases. This is a gift to the church, a tactile way to help us stay focused during prayer. I started to use this *chotki* in my morning prayer time, and holding on to it helped me stay focused. Legend has it that Saint Anthony designed the first *chotki* by using a leather string that he tied every time he prayed, but the devil came along and kept untying it, so he worked out a way to make a prayer rope that the devil couldn't untie!

Using the *chotki* brought me to the realization that holding other symbolic things as I pray enables me to stay focused. Since I spent seven and a half years of my life in Ibiza, I like to pray for the country every week, so I bought a small wooden holding cross and carved the word *Ibiza* into it. I hold it as I pray; it helps keep distraction at bay. At other times, I hold a round stone; this reminds me that God is my rock and helps me to pray that he will be a rock for others.

Physical objects are helpful as a reminder to pray

throughout the day too. I use a training exercise where I encourage people to find a marble and place it in their pocket; as they notice it there during the day, it prompts them to go to a quiet time in their head and pray for whatever or whoever the marble represents.

Despite my personal awkward moment, the string-knotting prayer exercise was very popular in St. Paul's Cathedral and became one of the tools 24–7 Prayer used when we later partnered with the Archbishop of Canterbury's prayer initiative Thy Kingdom Come. This simple idea has been used by thousands of people all around the world, and it's been beautiful to hear stories of individuals seriously committing to pray regularly for friends who have subsequently come to know Jesus. Is there power in any of the objects? Absolutely not. They are just aids to help us remain focused in prayer. I will use whatever is useful to help me stay present in the moment so that I don't end up wandering out of quiet time. Different things work at different times; be creative.

Breathing

Something we don't always pay attention to when we are praying is our breathing, but thinking about this can really help when it comes to distractions. The Jesus Prayer that I mentioned previously is what is known as a breathing prayer. Traditionally, you say *Lord Jesus Christ, Son of God* on the out breath and *have mercy on me* on the in breath. Greek Orthodox Bishop Kallistos Ware says of this prayer that within one short sentence are four consistent strands:

the cry for mercy, the discipline of repetition, the quest for stillness, and the veneration (worship and adoration) of the Holy Name.[6] All this in ten words!

As we pray, we seek the joy of mercy; we learn the discipline of repetition; we gain focus, find silence, and venerate the beautiful name of Jesus Christ. Of course, you don't have to use the words of the Jesus Prayer; you can find many inspiring Bible verses, or even compose your own phrases that help you to focus. In the ancient tradition, once monks had perfected the breathing prayer, they would utter just one word repeatedly. You can use these simple prayers anywhere, which allows you to easily pray and become aware of the presence of God wherever you are.

Posture

It's helpful to remember that we are whole systems—the physical and spiritual are not completely separate. Our posture in a quiet time can significantly affect us. I will often get up and walk around the room during a prayer time; the posture of standing and moving helps me focus. Some people find walking and praying so helpful that it's even better to go outside to do it. If I am particularly struggling with distraction, I might kneel to help me focus. I think I understand why people put their hands together when they pray—if nothing else, it stops us from fidgeting. It's good to think about the *way* we sit (or stand, or kneel, or walk . . .) as much as *where* we sit or stand or kneel or walk.

A helpful combination of posture and practicing the

tactile is a prayer exercise I use at the gym. I like to lift weights (not big ones, you understand), and when I bench-press with two weights in my hands, I give each weight the name of one of my two sons. As I lift the weights up, I symbolically and prayerfully lift my two sons up to God. I'm sure creative and fitter people can think of other prayerful exercises for the gym.

Summary

I regularly face the battle of distraction. I think it's something that everyone struggles with, even monks! Distraction comes on a good day, in a settled time, when life feels balanced and stable. Distractions usually increase at a time of change. Joining a different church, moving to a new home, starting your career, or making any other significant life change offers an ever-increasing number of windows to gaze out of.

The distraction may come from a genuine sense of doing something in the Kingdom of God, some act of Christian service, or simply trying to live missionally. Even in this, we need to be careful not to focus so much on building the Kingdom that we never take the time to sit at the feet of the King. To sit at his feet, we will need to challenge ourselves about distraction regularly, closing the windows that cause us to lose our focus on him.

We will need to be intentional: intentional in location, intentional in action, and intentional in interaction with the King.

Next time you pray and find yourself (inevitably) facing distraction, I encourage you to try one or more of the following:

- Name your distractions and tame them so they don't take over.

- Practice the tactile; try finding something to hold while you pray.

- Think about your breathing; find prayers and phrases that you can repeat in a rhythmic manner to help you to become calm and focused.

- Consider your physical posture.

In all this, keep in mind that the point is not to become prayer professionals but simply to, in the words of Jesus, "pray to your Father, who is unseen."

3

Scripture

MY LATE TEENS WERE TROUBLED YEARS while I tried and failed to cope with my mother's death. I found myself in trouble with the police on various occasions and was eventually sentenced to spend time in a probation hostel, where I awaited trial for another offense. During my time there, I began to recognize that I was stuck in a dysfunctional cycle that was not leading anywhere good. One morning, after a pretty hectic session of drug use, I finally acknowledged that I was at the end of my rope: broken, alone, and trapped. I picked up a Bible that had been given to me by some Christians a few weeks earlier and, sitting on my probation hostel bed, made an honest and sincere plea: *God, if you are real, save me.*

Letting the pages of the Bible fall open randomly, I read these words from the book of Isaiah: "Surely the arm of the LORD is not too short to save, nor his ear too dull to hear." I had prayed, *God, if you are real, save me,* and within moments I had read God's response. It leaped out at me, spoke to me, moved me—and I started to weep. In that moment, I gave my life back to God and committed to following him.

This afternoon, some thirty years on, I sat and held that same Bible, and it's a battered collection of papers again. It was one of those cheap paperback NIV Bibles that churches keep to give visitors; it's nothing outwardly special. But within its pages, I found life. That moment in the hostel will remain with me forever because God breathed on his Word; it became alive to me and changed the course of my existence—all in a moment! The power of this book is extraordinary.

A Lamp to Our Feet

Many years later I was a guest speaker at a London prison. One of the chaplaincy team members told me the story of a man who had discovered that the thin pages of his copy of the New Testament made perfect paper for his roll-up cigarettes. My colleague challenged him to at least read each page before he smoked it. By the time the man reached the book of John, he gave his life to Jesus. During a break I talked to another prisoner, who recited to us the only Bible verse he could remember. In the talk that followed, the speaker quoted that very verse; the guy looked around and wondered aloud whether the speaker was a mind reader! Prisoners and priests, winners and losers, kings and paupers have all been impacted by the power of the Bible, something I think is aptly referred to as the Word of God.

There are two things that every quiet time needs: prayer and the Bible. You can't separate the two. In the Psalms we read, "Your word is a light for my feet, a guide on my path" (119:105, PAR), and I have come to the conclusion that you will struggle to have an effective quiet time if it doesn't involve some Bible reading. You must approach the Bible with prayer, and you must approach prayer with the Bible. The order doesn't matter; sometimes I read before I pray, sometimes after I pray, but the Bible is always near me while I pray.

Gandhi, a man of Hindu faith, said, "You Christians look after a document containing enough dynamite to blow all civilization to pieces, turn the world upside down and bring peace to a battle-torn planet. But you treat it as though it is nothing more than a piece of literature."[1] He may have been generalizing, but I do understand the point he was trying to make! Surely it is important to read the sacred texts of our faith in their entirety if we are serious about growing in our faith. We need to give the Bible weight in our lives, allow it to challenge, inspire, and shape us and the way we live. And so we need to read it. Your private prayer place can become the greatest place to study the Bible.

The New York Public Library is home to a Gutenberg Bible, the first substantial book printed in the West, an amazing and almost priceless book. It is said that when the book arrived in New York in 1847, as it was brought into the customs house and carried through, everyone stood and took off their hats as a sign of respect for this remarkable book.

In Jewish synagogues, people stand to read the Scriptures; rabbis remain seated to give a sermon but stand to read the Scriptures. Jesus did the same; we read in Luke 4:16, "He went to Nazareth, where he had been brought up, and on the Sabbath day he went into the synagogue, as was his custom. He stood up to read." The Hebraic tradition was one that held the Scriptures with absolute respect. When I approach the Scriptures, I metaphorically take off my hat and stand in respect for what sits on my lap, next to my coffee!

For Christians, it is in the Bible that we often find the answers we are looking for. And yet, there are so many questions that can precede our reading of the Scriptures and prevent us from even starting in the first place.

Isn't It Boring?

My respect for the Bible is sincere, but I admit that there have been some times when I've found it hard going and—dare I even say it?—boring. If we approach the Bible and expect goosebumps every time we read it, we will be disappointed.

Perhaps it is possible to achieve profound revelation every time you read, but I don't want anyone to live with the illusion that everyone who recommends reading the Bible experiences a beautifully deep moment every time they pore over the ancient Scripture. There are days when you are in a hurry, the milk that you dribbled on your cornflakes was sour, or you slept in. Still, I have learned that I need to give the Bible consistent and regular time and approach reading it with a good attitude.

Won't It Make Me Religious?

I have heard a few people ask this, meaning *I don't want this to become a dull, lifeless routine, something I do out of a sense of obligation.* I fear that this could just hide a reluctance to commit to a routine. There are many other things that we know we will have to make routine space for in order to achieve certain outcomes that are important to us.

I think the word *religious* frightens us because of the negative way it's often been used. The word actually has its roots and meaning in "relating to or manifesting faithful devotion to an acknowledged ultimate reality or deity."[2] If that's what *religious* means, I want to be religious! I want to be faithfully devoted to God. I want to be faithfully devoted to growing in my understanding of God and to knowing him, and it seems to me that this will come about through prayer and reading the Bible.

What Version Should I Read?

There are more than four hundred different translations of the Bible into English. I read different versions from time to time because they give me a fresh perspective. If you always read the same version, it can be easy to read over familiar passages in autopilot mode. *The Message* translation can be a great starting point because a lot of study and care has been taken to word it in a really relatable way. From there, I believe we should progress to more weighty and detailed versions, definitely spending time in one that's been translated closely from the original language rather than paraphrased. Study Bibles with notes can be helpful for extra insight.

Whichever you read, I find that it's helpful to approach it with a highlighter and also to take notes so you can revisit things later. Don't be frightened to scribble all over your Bible—just don't scribble stuff out!

How Should I Approach Reading the Bible?

Get your head in the right space before you get the practicalities in the right place. When I look back on my probation hostel experience, I know that at that moment my head was in the right space: I was desperate. If I were to use the language of the Psalms, I would say that I was thirsty and hungry, parched and starving. I prayed a brief, one-line prayer, desperately challenging God to prove that he was real. Maybe if we always approach the Bible thirsty, hungry, and with prayer, we will be fed and refreshed every time we read it.

However we read the Bible in our quiet time, we need to do so prayerfully. Victorian preacher Charles Haddon Spurgeon said this about commentaries:

The commentators are good instructors, but the Author himself is far better, and prayer makes a

direct appeal to him and enlists him in our cause. It
is a great thing to pray one's self into the spirit and
marrow of a text: working into it by sacred feeding
thereon, even as the worm bores its way into the
kernel of the nut. Prayer supplies a leverage for the
uplifting of ponderous truths.[3]

I love that: "Prayer supplies a leverage for the uplifting of
ponderous truths." When I read I try to approach through
the gateway of stillness from Psalm 46:10, but I also use the
ancient refrain that Samuel used in the Tabernacle when God
spoke to him: "Speak, Lord, for Your servant is listening"
(1 Samuel 3:10, AMPC). If you are struggling to understand
what you are reading, pray. Ask God to illuminate the text
to you, to speak, to unfold the mystery. Sometimes this can
take days. Some verses that you read can prove difficult to
understand; in prayer you can work yourself into the text.
Try turning the verse into a prayer; sometimes I will write a
verse out or try to rewrite it in my own language to see if that
helps illuminate the Scripture. Or I will speak it out loud a
few times and try to turn it back to God.

How Should I Read the Bible, Practically Speaking?
Let's face it: You will be reading your Bible for years and
years, so it would be helpful to explore different ways of and
approaches to reading it. Many people use apps or reading
programs to help them read through the Bible in a year, and
I can't recommend these enough. Nicky Gumble's *Bible in*

One Year is incredibly helpful for anyone trying to develop a healthy, regular Bible-reading habit.

A basic premise is this: If you read four chapters of the Bible every day, you will read the entire Bible in one year. On average this would mean dedicating fifteen minutes of each day to Bible reading—or listening if you prefer.[4] Studies suggest that people spend an average of 147 minutes per day on social media. In case you missed the math, that's ten times more than the amount of time needed to read the Bible in a year.[5] I once challenged myself to read sixteen chapters a day so that I could read the entire Bible in just three months. It was a good challenge and, to complete it, I really did have to cut down on my social-media usage. I thought I'd attempt it a second time, but this time I felt the Lord challenge me on my attitude, saying, *It's not a competition, Brian!*

A question I often hear is *If you read so much, what do you get out of it?*—a question that carries more than a healthy dollop of consumeristic thinking! My friend Phil likens it to other healthy routines; he says, "I can't remember what I had for breakfast last Tuesday, but it was good for me." I try to eat a healthy breakfast every day because it is good for me; we should read the Bible every day because it is good for us.

Read Books in One Sitting

Another good thing to do would be to read whole books of the Bible in one reading. Mark is the shortest Gospel, taking around just two hours to read, so if I were going to read a whole Gospel in one go, that's where I'd start. It was actually intended to be read aloud communally when it was sent to the church in Rome in about AD 64 as the first-ever Gospel. I still marvel at the fact that those Roman Christians started a church and were willing to die for their faith under the persecution of Nero—and they didn't even have a Gospel in their first few years.

Read It Slowly

Some people are naturally drawn to the slow read. I have also adopted a one-chapter-a-day approach, which definitely slows the process down. I usually do this with a commentary within reach. Commentaries are really easy to download or quite cheap to buy, especially if you're happy with second-hand copies. So, for instance, if you are reading Genesis, you can find a commentary by some clever person who unpacks Genesis and read it as a companion to the book. This can be super illuminating and bring lots of new insights because commentators often explain cultural and historical context in a way that we don't automatically know.

Read It Yourself before Looking at a Commentary or Study Notes

I love study Bibles, but again, I think it's best to read a passage yourself and reflect to form your own thoughts on what it is saying before going to your study Bible notes or a commentary. Doing so allows the Scripture to be living and active and work in you before you have someone else's interpretation. I have moments of reassurance when I read a passage of Scripture and then find out that the commentator was thinking the same thoughts!

Summary

Andy Warhol, an American artist, once said, "It doesn't matter how slowly you go so long as you do not stop."[6] I think this is true of reading the Bible. Do not stop, do not let things get in your head when you miss a few days, do not imagine that God is angry, do not think that he is frustrated with you. The key is to keep going, even if it is slowly. Reading your Bible is not some "checkbox" exercise; it is about spending time with the truth, slowly finding out about and growing in relationship with the One we love.

Next time you read the Bible, you may want to keep one or more of the below in mind:

- Pray before you read.

- Find what works for you: time, place, how much you will read each day.

- Try reading a whole book at once, in one sitting (like Mark). Rather than searching for a few meaningful phrases, aim to come away with a general impression.

- Use audio versions of the Bible while driving or exercising.

- Buy or download a year-through-the-Bible reading plan.

- Find online sermons, commentaries, and study books about the text you are reading.

- Grab a pen and don't be afraid to scribble on (but not over) the Scriptures.

4

Memorize and Meditate

WHEN I WAS A YOUNG BOY, we had a slightly strange ritual for a while. My father would ask my brothers and me to memorize a Bible verse each day before we went to school. If we remembered the verse when we got home, we would be rewarded with sweets! I must have been about five years old and, even now, I remember the words of many of those verses but can't remember which sweets I had.

At my Sunday school, we played another game designed to help us find our way around the Bible. It was called Sword Drill, based on Hebrews 4:12, which says, "The word of God is alive and active. Sharper than any double-edged sword, it penetrates even to dividing soul and spirit, joints and marrow; it judges the thoughts and attitudes of the heart." The leader would issue the instruction "Draw swords!" (not as dangerous as it sounds), and we would all raise our Bibles, our swords, into the air. They would then give a Bible reference and suddenly shout "Charge!" which was our cue to frantically locate that place in the Bible, with the winner being the first to stand up and read the verse aloud. I loved it! And looking back, I also love that it was teaching us to remember passages of the Bible.

Bible verses implanted into my mind and heart through memory verses and Sword Drill have lived with me. Those verses have followed me around, almost haunting me in my dark days, and bringing me joy as I found the way back to God.

Memorize

My wife knows how to say "There was a young shepherd girl" in French because of a song she had to sing in school. How many of us still sing through the alphabet in our heads when we need to find something filed alphabetically? There could be a whole generation of children who still sing "Happy Birthday" when they wash their hands because that's what they were taught to do during the COVID-19 pandemic. Constant repetition instills things into our memories that we can easily draw on. Singing seems especially useful for this—it's one of the reasons I love worship songs that include words of Scripture. I believe there is something important about learning the sacred text of Scripture by heart.

In an age of GPS and smartphones, it appears that our memories are changing. Research by a Columbia University psychologist shows that

> since the advent of search engines, we are reorganizing the way we remember things. Our brains rely on the Internet for memory in much the same way they rely on the memory of a friend, family member or co-worker. We remember less through knowing information itself than by knowing where the information can be found.[1]

Instant access to information makes remembering less important. A term for this is *digital amnesia*. Instead of committing information to memory, we remember the place to find it, and increasingly, this is online. It has been said that when people lose their phones or can't get access to the internet, they sometimes suffer the same level of anxiety associated with losing a friend!

Personally, I love my devices, but have we ever become reliant on them! If I'm visiting someone now, I just ask for their address, but at one time I would call for directions, carefully writing down all the instructions. After a couple of visits, I would remember the way. We took several holidays in France when our children were young, navigating our way using a printed road atlas. Nowadays I travel all over the country and can't tell you how I got to where I was going—and without GPS, I wouldn't be able to find my way back.

I'm not saying this is wrong, simply that I rely on my device and not my memory to direct me.

A few years ago my wife and I traveled to Borneo, where we visited a tribe of ex-headhunters deep in the virgin rainforest. In an incredibly remote location with absolutely no internet access or phone signal, we would often find ourselves instinctively moving to show people a picture from social media and then realizing that without a signal we couldn't. Our devices have not only replaced our memories but have joined our conversations.

We no longer need to know our way around like we used to, but sometimes it's important that we can still find the way when the device isn't there. I use the Bible on my phone a lot, but it isn't a substitute for hiding God's Word in my heart. As the writer describes in Psalm 119:11, "I have hidden your word in my heart that I might not sin against you." How do we hide his Word in our hearts?

When we talk of the "heart," we refer to who we are at the core. Most of the time when *heart* is mentioned in the Bible, it means so much more than the myogenic muscular organ that is found in all mammals! Greek scholar Dr. Gleason Archer explained that the Greeks would have understood *heart*, or *kardia*, to mean the "'desire-producer that makes us tick,' and the source of our 'desire-decisions' that establish who we really are."[2] Professor William Thayer described this Greek view of the heart as "the fountain and seat of the thoughts, passions, desires, appetites, affections, purposes, endeavors."[3] Our heart could be described as the center of who we are, the place from where our purpose comes, where we find our identity, and where we nurture our values; it's here that we need to memorize and hide God's Word.

What's the Verse That Helps You through the Storm?

Mark 4 recounts a great story about Jesus and his disciples crossing the Sea of Galilee on a boat. A large storm blows up and, surprisingly, a group of seasoned fishermen panic, indicating that this was an alarming situation. They wake the unscared and sleeping Jesus, who stands up and commands, "Peace, be still" (Mark 4:39, KJV). The storm calms instantly, and then Jesus rebukes his disciples for not having enough faith. I've wondered about that rebuke—it seems a bit harsh to tell someone off when they've clearly just been terrified. I wonder if he rebuked them because he had said to them, "Let us go over to the other side" (Mark 4:35). This was a statement from the Son of God and, therefore, was the Word of God. In fact, the earlier part of the same chapter is all about the Word of God.

Many years ago, I heard renowned Christian John Wimber speak about this story. He suggested that perhaps Jesus rebuked the disciples for their lack of faith because they forgot either the Word of God or power of the One who spoke. In the middle of a storm, the disciples forgot what was important; they forgot that if Jesus said "Let us go to the other side," that was what was going to happen. They hadn't "hidden it in their hearts"; they forgot what he had said.

When trouble comes, when storms erupt, having the Word of God in our lives is very important. What Bible verses have we committed to memory that we can draw on when storms come? When I lie awake at night, troubled or anxious, what verses can I call to mind to bring peace and calm?

Hanging on the wall in my parents' home is an old, printed Scripture that says, "And we know that all things work together for good to them that love God, to them who are the called according to his purpose" (Romans 8:28, KJV). I know it has sustained my father through the loss of his first wife, my mother, to cancer. These words have also sustained me in times when life hasn't seemed to be going as planned.

When we moved to Spain as missionaries, we didn't have a fixed income, and there were times when we felt the financial pressure and could get a little fearful. Then we would recall Matthew 6:25, which says, "I tell you, do not worry about your life, what you will eat or drink; or about your body, what you will wear. Is not life more than food, and the body more than clothes?" This became our verse for the storm.

You will need multiple verses to help you face the storms of life; if they are "hidden in your heart," they will sustain and strengthen you. God says,

> As the rain and the snow
>   come down from heaven,
> and do not return to it
>   without watering the earth

and making it bud and flourish,
   so that it yields seed for the sower and bread
      for the eater,
so is my word that goes out from my mouth:
   It will not return to me empty,
but will accomplish what I desire
   and achieve the purpose for which I sent it.

ISAIAH 55:10-11

God's Word doesn't return empty.

Pick some verses and start to commit them to memory. In my quiet time I will often repeatedly write out a verse from memory so that I get to know it. Recently I've memorized Romans 15:13: "May the God of hope fill you with all joy and peace as you trust in him, so that you may overflow with hope by the power of the Holy Spirit." As I wrote amid the global pandemic, this was my verse of hope for that storm.

At the back of most Bibles are guides with key verses, or you could even google "top ten verses to memorize"! Try committing one to memory in the morning and see if you can recall it in the evening.

Meditate

What does the word *meditation* mean to you? Some see it as spiritually dangerous or discount it as simply not for them. In reality, meditation has deep roots in the Christian faith. Psalm 1 sets a precedent for Christians regarding meditation. Originally written as an encouragement to the children of

Israel to meditate on the Word of God, this simple psalm reveals that there is life and fruitfulness to be found for those who meditate on the Word "day and night."

> Blessed is the one
>   who does not walk in step with the wicked
> or stand in the way that sinners take
>   or sit in the company of mockers,
> but whose delight is in the law of the LORD,
>   and who meditates on his law day and night.
> That person is like a tree planted by streams of water,
>   which yields its fruit in season
> and whose leaf does not wither—
>   whatever they do prospers.

PSALM I:I-3

The word *meditate* used in this psalm denotes a "verbalized rumination," like a pigeon cooing repetitively, a gentle murmuring.[4] The same word is also linked to mastication. This is chewing the cud—the process by which a cow eats grass in such a way as to extract all the nutrients. Perhaps it's easier to think of it like sucking a hard sweet rather than crunching it; if we suck the sweet, we allow all the flavors to coat our mouth and end up fully tasting the sweet. Sometimes in my daily Bible reading I can crunch my way through the text rather than stopping to meditate and absorb the full flavor of what I am reading.

Therefore, meditation is not an emptying of one's mind,

as some people fear, but a filling of one's mind and thoughts with the Word of God. Repeating the Word of God, like the murmuring of a cooing pigeon, allows the Bible to fully permeate our senses and become embedded in our hearts. We can meditate on the Word of God by simple repetition of a biblical phrase, passage, or verse.

Another way to get a real sense of having the Bible embedded in your heart would be to practice *lectio divina*, which, translated from Latin, is simply "divine reading." The early church pioneers practiced this as a way of getting into the text and allowing the text to get into them. This helpful ancient practice is about reading Scripture in order to encounter God. It is not really about the sort of deep theological exploration and dissection of the biblical text that you might carry out for a Bible study.

There are four movements to *lectio divina*: *Read, Meditate, Pray,* and *Act.* Enter into this time through the gateway of Psalm 46:10, which we talked about in the first chapter: "Be still, and know that I am God."

1. *Read.* Read the passage in a slow and measured way. Read it more than once, maybe three or four times. Try to get a sense of what is happening and who is speaking. Take your time.

2. *Meditate.* Think about it, allowing the flavor of the text to seep out. Don't try to insert too much meaning at first; mull it over and see what God draws to

the surface. Approach this prayerfully, asking the Holy Spirit to be with you, trusting that illumination will come. Don't rush it. Ponder, weigh, consider.

3. *Pray.* You've allowed God to speak to you through the text; now it's your turn to speak to him. Have a simple conversation with him about what you have just read: Explain how it made you feel, what you noticed as you read.

4. *Act.* Identify how you might need to respond. Sometimes this will be a specific action to take; sometimes it might be a shift in attitude or behavioral pattern that needs to be addressed; sometimes it will simply be a reassurance to continue on a path you've already decided to follow.

This is a simple way to approach the Bible and will help in hiding God's Word in your heart. Lectio 365 is an app developed by 24–7 Prayer, which is designed to help people go on this journey with Scripture every day. We use the acronym *PRAY* for this, which is incredibly similar to the process above: *Pause, Reflect, Ask, Yield.* I highly recommend it.

Summary
Memorizing and meditating sit very well together and often blend into one another. As we memorize Scripture, we meditate on it. And as we meditate on Scripture, we memorize it. Here are some simple steps to get started.

- Pick a Bible verse to memorize this week at the beginning of the day; see if you can remember it in the evening—rewarding yourself with sweets is optional!

- Write a Bible phrase, passage, or verse on a Post-it Note and stick it somewhere where you will see it several times during the course of your day: on your phone or computer screen, on the bathroom mirror, on the fridge door, in your car—anywhere prominent. Each time you see it, take a moment to meditate on it.

- Set aside thirty minutes of one of your quiet times this week to practice *lectio divina* as described above.

- Our 24–7 Prayer staff team exchange "verses of the week" in our meeting every Friday. Find someone else that you can do this with—either digitally or in person. It really is just as simple as asking each other "What was your verse of the week?"

5

Journaling

"SOMETIMES YOU'RE FURTHER THAN THE MOON / Sometimes you're closer than my skin."[1]

The first time I heard these lyrics, I was deeply impacted. I was moved that someone had managed to articulate how it really felt to have a relationship with God. The bravery and authenticity of these lines touched me; the honest observation that at times it feels like God is close and at other times it feels like he is distant resonated with my own experience. At the time those lyrics were new and fresh to me, but I have become increasingly aware that lyricists, poets, authors, church pioneers, and even the writers of the Bible have been employing this kind of honesty for years. And that was exactly what it was about the lyrics that struck me—their honesty.

Over twenty years later, at the age of forty-nine, while in a position of senior Christian leadership, I managed to articulate to God how I really felt with an equally honest phrase. In one journal entry, I could only find six words to describe the kind of month I'd been having, and one was an expletive. The phrase I used would never be put in a worship song, and it definitely wouldn't be sung on a Sunday morning! I had been struggling with my mental health, and projects I was working on were proving to be clunky, taxing, and a little bit draining. I had a few relational tensions, I was traveling a lot, I was tired and eating too much. When I sat down to write my prayer to God in a journal, this phrase was all that came out. I'm even nervous putting it here, but I think we have to understand that God can cope with our honesty, even if we verbalize it in a less than eloquent way. William Wordsworth sums it up very well when he says, "Fill your paper with the breathings of your heart."[2] That is how my heart felt at the time, and it came across on the page of my journal in this crude and basic manner. I breathed out my brokenness; I tried to articulate the state of my heart, trusting that God could cope with my explicit honesty. Sometimes all we can summon is a guttural, basic cry, which I know God will hear. God already knows our hearts, as 1 Samuel 16:7 tells us: "People look at the outward appearance, but the LORD looks at the heart." He knows our hearts, what we are thinking, feeling, and going through. I believe it is helpful and therapeutic to access our hearts and express what is going on by writing it down. This practice is called journaling.

Maybe you've journaled for a long time; maybe you have

not previously considered adding it into your spiritual practices. Journaling in the context of a quiet time is the practice of processing our thoughts and connecting with God by writing or drawing in a journal. Honesty is key to journaling; this practice is not for show.

Have you ever read Psalm 109? It doesn't make it into a lot of sermons and isn't included in the lectionary. It's brutal, but it's honest; it gives insight into David's anger, frustration, and annoyance with his enemies as he lists the ways he would like God to treat his enemies.

> Appoint someone evil to oppose my enemy;
>   let an accuser stand at his right hand.
> When he is tried, let him be found guilty,
>   and may his prayers condemn him.
> May his days be few;
>   may another take his place of leadership.
> May his children be fatherless
>   and his wife a widow.
> May his children be wandering beggars;
>   may they be driven from their ruined homes.
> May a creditor seize all he has;
>   may strangers plunder the fruits of his labor.
> May no one extend kindness to him
>   or take pity on his fatherless children.
> May his descendants be cut off,
>   their names blotted out from the next generation.

PSALM 109:6-13

As a friend of mine once said, the Bible is more honest about prayer than most churches!

We don't know if God actually answered David's prayer here by doing what he asked, but I love that the Bible contains prayers with this level of brutal honesty. It makes me chuckle when I try to imagine someone praying something like Psalm 109 in a prayer meeting; people would be concerned, and someone would probably arrange to have a chat with them about forgiveness. These kinds of prayers are probably better expressed in a journal than in a public place, but I believe that King David shows us that you need not pull punches when it comes to revealing the honest state of your heart before the Maker of heaven and earth.

Start Small

My first journal was a very small (four-by-four-inch) book I bought in 1996. And though you don't have to use a book that is literally small in size, I do think it is good with journaling to start small, especially if you find the idea unfamiliar or daunting. When I started to journal, I would write a few Bible verses or a prayer, and then I would jot down a few thoughts about the youth work we were leading at that time. I found it really helpful to process what we were doing in the youth work and also to gain some self-awareness of how I was doing personally and in my leadership. It was simple; it was lots of short phrases and one-line prayers. Starting small has naturally developed into much more developed writing, and though there are no hard-and-fast rules, a lot of the practices I write about in this book will be greatly enhanced by journaling.

What Should You Use?

For years, while living in Ibiza, I kept a blog, which was effectively my journal. Looking back, I can see that at times I treated it as if it was my personal journal, writing frankly and without filters; at other times, I was aware that people were reading it, so I started to be a touch more guarded. Using digital media to keep a journal is good, but it can come with unhelpful pressure if you make it public! Similarly, there is a benefit to the immediacy of journaling on a phone or tablet, but the downside is the distraction of messages pinging in at a time when you're trying to focus.

For me, I think it can be helpful to have a physical book that you write in. There is something fresh about stepping away from the screen and putting pen or pencil to paper. I buy a lot of my journals in charity shops and thrift stores, which can be a bit random because occasionally you buy a book in which someone has written a few pages! I also like that when I write on paper, there is no delete button; my unrefined, honest thoughts are recorded in their unedited form. Whatever medium you choose for journaling, bear in mind that it doesn't have to be elaborate. Whether it's a basic Word document, a simple reporter's notebook, or a hand-stitched leather journal doesn't matter.

When Should You Journal?

Personally, I try to write daily because that can be really helpful when you are trying to establish it as a habit. In the long term, you won't always feel the need to write every day; for me, I find that this is seasonal. Some people find that daily journaling isn't ideal for them and prefer to write a longer entry perhaps once a week. Some people write at the end of the day to process all that has happened; others prefer to write at the beginning of the day. Regardless of the time of day, there are no rules on grammar or content by which your journal will be assessed! It doesn't matter whether an entry is a single sentence or an epic, twenty-page monologue. Your literary style is unimportant. It's just a case of writing something.

Whom Do You Address It To?

When I write in my journal as part of my quiet time, I tend to write as if writing to God, which makes it a prayer. At other times, I'm processing thoughts, writing quotes, or doodling about something I have read or heard, which doesn't really feel like prayer. This is more me writing to myself, trying to make sense of my world, but I always work with the assumption that God is looking at what I write and leading me in it.

What Should You Write About?

Record Bible Verses

I find it beneficial to write out verses from the Bible. It's another helpful tool in memorizing them, and taking time to write also makes you pause and think about the words. Sometimes I underline the verse in my Bible and write it in my journal. Sometimes I spot a theme that is emerging in my Bible reading over a few days; this gets my attention and makes me wonder what God is trying to communicate to me.

I'm fascinated by how often I have written a verse in my journal and then heard that same verse preached about or shared in a meeting soon after. When this happens, I go back to my journal entry and look again at what God might be saying to me. First Samuel 3 tells the story of God speaking to the young boy Samuel in the Tabernacle; he calls him three times. This shows me that God is happy to repeat himself. Hearing the same theme expressed in multiple ways is often the Lord being repetitive so that we hear what he is saying. When I write such things down, I more easily notice the repetitions and reflect on the voice of God.

Write in Your Bible

Or, to flip the process completely, you could actually write in your Bible. It is really helpful to underline or annotate verses or elaborate on them in your own words. Bible journaling is also good for writing down dates and times next to verses that have spoken to you or putting people's names next to specific verses for prayer. You can even buy journaling Bibles that have extra-wide blank margins in them specially designed for you to write in.

Explore and Record Bible Themes

Occasionally I will give myself specific exercises. For example: Find all the recorded prayers of Paul and write about each one. Jesus asks lots of questions in the Gospels; make a note of them and add your thoughts on what he asks and the responses he receives. Or identify the amazing promises God makes to Abraham in the book of Genesis and think about their significance and power. This kind of journaling helps you understand more about God as well as yourself. Journaling in conjunction with *lectio divina*, which we talked about in the previous chapter, works really well.

Write Thoughts

Writing can help you process your emotions and learn to understand yourself. A few years ago, I realized by looking back through my journal that a pattern had emerged. I noticed that every time I got back from overseas travel, I would question whether I was in the right job. For three days I would be thinking, *Should I be looking to serve the Lord in a different way?* But after five days I would stop thinking this way. Basically, I was travel weary, and I soon learned that after a long overseas trip was not the time to think about my future. Journaling will help us discover unhelpful thoughts and patterns in our lives.

Practice Gratitude

There is an increasing trend of journaling and well-being bloggers encouraging us to be thankful. I wholeheartedly agree that thankfulness boosts our mood and helps keep us mentally healthy. For me, this trend could be enhanced by being thankful *to* someone. So I use my journal to express gratitude to God. There's an old hymn with these lyrics:

> *Count your many blessings, name them one by one,*
> *And it will surprise you what the Lord has done.*
> *Count your blessings, name them one by one;*
> *Count your blessings, see what God hath done.*[3]

A review of the years, months, weeks, or days that have passed will help you see the hand of God in your life and build gratitude into your devotions. If you are feeling particularly negative, it's a good challenge to spend half an hour writing about the things you are grateful for. I guarantee that this will lift your spirit and make you feel more positive.

At specific times in the year, I deliberately use my journal as a time to reflect on the goodness of God. Every New Year's, I try to write a thankful review for the year that has just passed, expressing gratitude for people, experiences, and places that have had an impact on me. When I reached the age of fifty, I decided to write a sentence for each year of my life that reflected back to God my gratitude for his presence, seen and unseen, throughout the years. You can review any season or significant moment in this way. Graduations, wedding anniversaries, children's birthdays, funerals—any of these can be a good opportunity to review, notice the emotions you feel, and give thanks.

Pray through History

Making a note of major events happening in the world at the time of a journal entry is something I have found useful—perhaps not so much at the time, but certainly when I look back through what I have written. It helps to give context to the thoughts I have recorded. For example, one of my journal entries notes, "Today the UK voted to leave the EU"; it's useful to know that this significant moment influenced the words I wrote on that day and to think about how God has worked since then. Our quiet times should never be detached from the realities of the world we live in, so noting what those are when we journal is helpful.

Write Specific Prayers

When I am particularly concerned for someone or I find that they are often on my mind, I find it helpful to write a specific prayer to God in my journal just for that person. In the process of writing, I think more clearly about what it is that I really want to ask God to do for them when I speak my prayer. Being able to go back to the prayer and repeat it, or even add to it, also feels significant. I have sometimes come across powerful or inspiring prayers written by others; I write those in my journal, too, and I pray them myself from time to time. I have specific prayers for family members and friends that I fall back on often.

Journaling for Others

A number of years ago, I began to realize that both my sons would one day leave home. Part of me never really wanted them to go—I love their company and really enjoy hanging out with them. But I knew that they would leave, that it was important for them that they become independent. I started thinking about what I wanted to give them that would be significant—other than my love and cash! So, for each of them, I read a Bible all the way through and made notes in it that I hoped would be helpful, and then I gave it to them when they left. I have two sons, and my only regret was that I wished I had started journaling for them earlier. If you are a parent, one day your children will leave home. One of the most beautiful things you could give them would be a Bible that you have annotated and journaled in, that will perhaps stick with them for the rest of their lives. A well-journaled Bible could become a heritage piece and a legacy that you leave for your family. (It doesn't have to be for your children; there may be other people you would like to give this kind of gift to.)

Poetry

I once heard someone say we should read more poetry because it is difficult to read quickly. Poetry has often felt a little ethereal for me, something that has beauty but lacks substance. My view on this has changed over the years. I like reading poetry and have also tried my hand at writing poetry in my journal (most of it not fit for publication!). Remember, it's all about the honesty, not the quality. Sometimes a journaled poem is more a stream of consciousness than a carefully crafted and constructed piece.

Drawing

In a similar fashion, drawing as part of journaling can be incredibly freeing. You engage a different part of your brain when you draw or doodle, and I find that this is a helpful way of processing and focusing on the Lord. For example, I have drawn a tightly closed hand and imagined myself in the palm of God's hand; I have drawn a tree and considered verses that speak about God's nourishment and being under his shade.

Again, the quality of your drawing is not important. Even if you don't consider yourself to be particularly artistic, there is a place for art in your journal. Over the years we have seen 24–7 Prayer rooms across the globe populated by prayers that have been drawn and painted. I have no doubt that some of these beautiful and inspiring images started in someone's journal, and the role of imagination in our quiet times is so important that I've dedicated the whole next chapter to it.

Summary

The key to all journaling is honesty; this is something that is normally between you and God. Sometimes honesty with God will mean trying to get beyond the initial words and digging into your feelings. I often start with blandness; it almost feels like a catch-up, a short note to a friend, but as I continue to write, as I persevere, I access my feelings. Strangely, as I go deeper, my handwriting gets untidier; the deeper I go, the faster I write. It flows, but it gets messy.

Honest prayer and lament won't surprise God or even hurt his feelings. He is looking for your transparency and will meet you in the midst of the questions, fears, and doubts that can sometimes almost seem wrong to think. The process of writing them out and talking to God about them will help you to live an honest and secure life before him. David writes in Psalm 116:1, "I love the LORD, because he has heard my voice and my pleas for mercy" (ESV). A journal will help you find your voice in prayer and will also give you a faithful record of your journey with the Lord. There is real joy to be found in journaling; it offers the chance to reflect, to process, to pray, and to come to terms with yourself and God in your quiet time. I look at the journal I am writing today and the one from twenty-five years ago, and I can see that God has heard my voice—at times honest, angry, broken, but heard.

- If you have been journaling for some time, why don't you spend some time reflecting back over the previous weeks or months or even what was happening this time last year? What has God been speaking to you about or doing in your life?

- If you have never journaled before, why not start small? Grab a piece of paper or a book and begin by writing a prayer to God.

6

Imagination

JESUS WAS A MASTER STORYTELLER. He often taught using parables. The four Gospels record forty-six occasions when Jesus used a story to teach a lesson. He used simple, culturally relevant stories that engaged the listeners' imaginations to illuminate a spiritual truth. He revealed the heart and nature of God to his listeners through these parables.

As people listened, they could visualize exactly what Jesus was talking about; they would be fully engaged, picturing the many day-to-day objects, people, situations, and activities that Jesus referred to. As Jesus told his stories, those who listened engaged their imaginations, perhaps picturing themselves in the settings he described. Just as this helped them to understand the point Jesus was trying to make, our imaginations will help us when it comes to engaging with the stories in the Bible.

We have looked at mindwandering and how we can be so easily distracted in a quiet time, but I want to look at the other side of the coin and explore how imagination can help us connect with God. During a lecture, N. T. Wright once said:

> I have debated in public in America with colleagues in the New Testament guild who refuse to believe in the bodily resurrection and, again and again, the bottom line is when they say, "I just can't imagine that," the answer is "Smarten up your imagination." And the way to do that is not to beat them over the head with dogma but so to create a world of mystery and beauty and possibility that actually there are some pieces of music which when you come out of them it is much easier to say "I believe in the Father and the Son and the Holy Spirit" than when you went in.[1]

This is such a simple yet profound response. How do we "smarten up" our imaginations? How does my imagination become a useful tool in developing an understanding of God and a useful means of encountering him?

The imagination can be a powerful tool when activated well during a quiet time. There are so many ways we can approach the Bible. As I have mentioned, the use of commentaries and looking at what Bible scholars say often sheds light on context and brings interpretation to the Bible, which is insightful and life-giving. But this should not lead us to conclude that textual analysis is solely an affair of the mind and not the heart. We could get so caught up in looking at the original intent of the author and trying to place the passage in historical context that we'd forget that there are other ways to approach Scripture that require more imagination and a different approach to the ancient texts.

The Power of Image

Images speak to us. Whether they are in paintings, photographs, movies, or television shows, we are all impacted by images. You have only to look at Instagram to see this. Looking at images is an important part of our lives. The first camera offered for sale commercially was a Kodak in 1888, and since then photography has been an ever-increasing pastime. It has been estimated that approximately 1.4 trillion photos were taken in 2020—that's the equivalent to every person on the planet, 7.9 billion people, taking about 190 photos each!

For thousands of years before photography, we relied on paintings; this form of art was the predominant way images were captured. I have always been fascinated by painting and have loved visiting galleries since I was a boy. In fact, during a particularly difficult period of my life, when I was homeless,

I spent many hours in the National Gallery in London. I would gaze at the paintings and experience a measure of peace in the midst of the turbulence I felt in my life and my mental health. I was often drawn to religious paintings. For years I found it perplexing that these paintings weren't a true representation of what people would have looked like in Jesus' time. For instance, if you look at paintings by Italian Renaissance or Baroque artists painted in the sixteenth and seventeenth centuries, you will notice that all the people look Italian. It doesn't feel right. I wondered if some prejudice caused them to move away from the Aramaic appearance of Middle Eastern Christians to create a more palatable Italian version. As we delve further into why this happened, there is perhaps a stranger and more interesting explanation that will help us explore our use of imagination, one that has more to do with imaginative engagement than cultural misrepresentation.

Let us look at the Italian artist Caravaggio and arguably one of his greatest paintings, *The Supper at Emmaus*. There are two paintings with the same title, one of which happens to be at the National Gallery in London. This is one of the paintings I have spent the most time looking at. It's a beautiful painting that captures the moment when Christ is revealed to two disciples, after his crucifixion and resurrection, while he breaks bread in a pub. You can read the full story in Luke 24:13-35. There is a warmheartedness and depth to this painting, which depicts a beautiful, deep light breaking from the left, capturing the surprise of the revelation of a risen Christ in the expression and hand movements of the disciples. One of my friends says, "It's all about the hands," but I think there is more to it.

For me, it's all about the light. Caravaggio's use of *chiaroscuro*, meaning "light and dark," captures the mood and moment beautifully. In the painting, light dispels darkness, yet shadow remains; the light is dispelling fear and illuminating hope as the two disciples express shock at the revelation of Christ. The shadow makes the light appear to shine more brightly. Jesus is revealed with rather cherubic features, possibly because Caravaggio was one of the few early painters who painted Jesus without a beard! As Sister Wendy Beckett puts it,

> *The Supper at Emmaus* still has its power to shock, with the strangely "unspiritual" Christ, a youth with plump, pointed face and loose locks, unbearded and undramatic. Why should Christ not look like this? The unpretentious face allows the drama to be inherent in the event.[2]

It's a stunning piece of work, allowing Christ to be revealed to us as he comes into the darkness of our own lives with light, life, and hope.

The painter Caravaggio was a troubled soul. In his early years as an artist, he was deeply influenced by a Milanese cardinal called Borromeo, who himself was deeply influenced by Saint Ignatius of Loyola, a Franciscan monk.[3] Saint Ignatius wanted people to approach the Bible in an imaginative way. John Goldingay says,

> Modern interpretation assumed that biblical narrative was history, with the high boredom potential of that designation. Ignatian interpretation assumes that biblical narrative is story—not that it did not happen, but that we need to enter into it as story, into the lives of the characters and the unfolding of the scene, and find our place there.[4]

Cardinal Borromeo wanted people to enter into the story, so he asked painters to paint biblical events in such a way that people could picture themselves in the scene. Initially, this was around the crucifixion of Christ, but it developed and grew.

When we understand this, we can better understand Caravaggio's *Supper at Emmaus*. He invites the person looking at the painting into the story. The scene is set in a tavern or inn; the innkeeper hasn't removed his hat, which suggests that this was an unrefined establishment. The disciples are shabby and poor; one has a torn jacket. They are also pilgrims, men on a journey, which is indicated by a shell on one man's garment. The scene depicts ordinary men sitting in an ordinary pub, encountering an extraordinary God. For me the most striking image is the plate of food jutting out from the edge of the table at the front of the painting. It speaks to me: It tells me that I can come and sit at this table; it invites me to access the room and be part of the drama. Christ wants to reveal himself to me, to sit and eat with me. My imagination is engaged, and I am drawn into the story. Revelation 3:20 springs to mind: "Here I am! I stand at the door and knock. If anyone hears my voice and opens the door, I will come in and eat with that person, and they with me." This work is saying, "You are part of this story. Come and take your place at the table."

This vivid use of painting in a time of poor literacy was tremendously helpful for people to understand Scripture and also to better understand God. But you may be wondering how all that helps us in the here and now. The world around us today looks quite different from how it would have in Jesus' time on earth, but just as these men—Ignatius, Borromeo, Caravaggio—influenced people in their time to visualize themselves in a setting that was different from their own experience, we can also try to place ourselves in the stories of the Bible.

Try This as an Exercise

1. Find a passage from one of the Gospels where Jesus is connecting with or spending time with other people. This could, perhaps, be one of the miraculous events or a discourse as they walk along a dusty road. It doesn't matter if the incident is long or short, but at this point, it would be good to have Jesus in it.

2. Remember that you are engaging with and encountering the Word of God. Remember that the Word of God brings life and has power. Think about the Gutenberg Bible being brought into New York and metaphorically take your hat off and stand as you approach it!

3. Be still and remember God is present. You need God to illuminate what you are about to read. It is helpful to prayerfully acknowledge his presence by saying a simple *Thank you, God, that you are here.*

4. Name and tame any distractions and think about your breathing and posture.

5. Read through the passage three or more times, until you start to become familiar with the story. Try to picture the details.

6. Once you have this passage pretty well locked in, it's time to move to the main part of the exercise. I have a super active imagination and like the idea of constructing a movie-like setup. Some people take a more verbal approach or mull over some specifics. It is helpful to remember this: "Vividness is not a criterion for the effectiveness of this kind of prayer. Engagement is, and the result is a more interior knowledge of Jesus."[5]

   • Close your eyes and reconstruct the scene in your imagination; take your time and try to move through the scene chronologically.

- Observe what is happening. Watch the people—the children, women, and men in the scene.
- Ask yourself questions like these: *What time of day is it? What temperature is it? Are people tired? What are the environmental conditions like? Is there a lot of noise? What can you smell? What does Jesus look like? How are other people reacting to and interacting with him? What are people chatting about among themselves? Is there emotion in their words—sadness, anger, curiosity, joy, judgment? Is Jesus doing anything specific? Who is he focusing on? Who is he praying for, and what does that look like?*

7. Place yourself in the scene in whatever way you want—as a member of the crowd, a person receiving healing, one of the disciples, a friend of the person needing healing. Probably best not to make yourself Jesus—we don't want anyone coming out of this with a Messiah complex!

8. When you have finished this time, it is helpful to pray, to speak with Jesus. Express your heart, what you have seen and felt from this time, what you've observed, what's made you happy, what's made you sad, what other emotions you've felt. Helmut Gabel says, "Every meditation ends with a prayer of colloquy, 'speaking personally, as one friend speaks to another, or as a servant to his master.'"[6]

9. Writing about your encounter in your journal will be helpful if you have time.

7

Wonder

"Attention is the beginning of devotion," wrote American poet Mary Oliver.[1] We live in a world in which our attention is constantly being demanded. In an environment driven by consumerism, advertisers communicate that we should always look for and aspire to more. Phone providers, streaming services, news outlets, national retail chains, charities, and social media are all clamoring for our attention, telling us we won't be satisfied until we have achieved certain goals, purchased certain products, or adopted a certain look. Is it a coincidence that once we get close to achieving the goals, they all shift and change?

Our attention is constantly diverted. We keep reaching

false summits only to find that there is a new one to climb. Inwardly we are sick of it; deep down we know what is happening. But on another level we embrace the narrative that says, "You will be happy when . . ."

And it's not solely the material that grabs our attention. *I'll be happy when I'm independent, when I get to travel, when I get the recognition I've been looking for, when I meet a partner, when I have my own place, when I get a bigger place,* and on and on and on.

There is a drum beating in our culture, and it beats to a rhythm that says: next, next, next. Our heads are spinning, our attention is constantly shifting, and our devotion gets pulled in all sorts of directions. We barely have time to stop and look up!

Stop and Look Up
When we had a prayer space in St. Paul's Cathedral, it was set up in St. Michael's Chapel, which is near the front door. In the process of setting up a prayer space, you can quickly become very busy with lots of practical tasks, especially when the space is set in a national historic building with only a small window of time before the public comes in. As often happens, we realized we had forgotten something, this time an extension cable. We were told that the building caretaker had one we could use. I quickly walked the length of the building, past the Duke of Wellington's final resting place, to an office where the caretaker might be, only to be told that he was downstairs. I rushed down, passing Admiral Lord

Nelson's final resting place. (The place is full of resting places, but I certainly wasn't getting any rest as I charged about!) Arriving downstairs, I found out that the caretaker had gone back up another way. I sighed and charged back upstairs. I was busy, I was focused, and I was starting to become a little bit flustered.

Then in a moment, something deep within me said, *Stop and look up.* I was standing below the beautiful domed ceiling of St. Paul's Cathedral, an architectural and artistic wonder of vibrant colors, glorious artwork, and stunning design. In my busyness I hadn't paused once. Intent on getting the job done, I had not stopped to look up and notice the beauty all around me.

Perhaps on that day in particular I needed the point to be emphasized. We had borrowed a kneeler for the prayer space and had placed a lovely leather-bound journal on it so that people could kneel and write their prayers. A member of the church staff quickly bustled over and said, "Ah, I see you have used Her Majesty's kneeler." I had apparently requisitioned the Queen of England's kneeler for our prayer activity. Embarrassed, I explained that I hadn't noticed; the staff member said to me, "You need to look up." Right above where the kneeler had previously been positioned was the royal crest. The staff graciously covered the kneeler with a cloth, and I smiled every time I saw people kneel on it that week, addressing the King of kings from the Queen of England's kneeler.

Later that week I wrote in my journal, "Lord, I continue

to seek you; I increasingly want to be at a place of consistent God consciousness. But the day creeps in, work moves along, and before I know it, I haven't stopped to catch my breath to see you, to touch base with you. Sometimes there is a hurried moment, but I need to do more than that: I need to stop and look up." I had become distracted, and what I was learning in the quiet time wasn't being realized in the day-to-day. The feeling of the chair wasn't coming with me!

I decided I was going to be more intentional with my attention. I was going to start looking for God—to slow down, notice, and give my attention to him. I challenged myself to write in my journal where I had seen God the previous day. I aimed to look for him in the ordinary, not the spectacular. One day I wrote this:

I see you in my sons—their banter, their fun, their discovery of you. I see you in my wife—her diligence, her care for our visitors, her concern for others. I hear you in my son's guitar playing that rings throughout the house. I saw your provision for my other son in getting his hard drive fixed by a friend—you are a God of generous friendships. I saw you in *The Blue Planet*, the beauty of your creation. I saw you as I fixed a painting for Tracy's parents—you restore what's been damaged. I saw you in the faces of so many wonderful people at church yesterday. Lord, help me to look for you more, to notice you.

Wonder is the ability to stop and look up. Wonder is a feeling of amazement and admiration, caused by something beautiful, remarkable, or unfamiliar.

Have Instagram and other photographic and image-rich media robbed us of the ability to wonder at the ordinary so that life only looks good when we see it through a filter? People project perfect online profiles, with flawless skin, perfect makeup, and pristine loungewear. They present a recipe idea while simultaneously performing dance moves with their chiseled boyfriend, who is repurposing an old van into a luxurious camper for travel to all the waterfalls in Iceland. A filtered life can rob us of wonder. If we are not careful, our appreciation of what is beautiful becomes distorted. Our definition of *beauty* needs an overhaul. There is beauty in toast, in wrinkled skin, in industrial skylines. There is beauty in barren deserts. There is beauty in hospitals. There is beauty in rust.

I remember one night in August 1987 when I had left home and decided to travel to Ireland with a friend. We missed the last ferry crossing and spent the night in a little café near the dock, where most of the customers were prostitutes. We sat for hours drinking, smoking, and chatting, nothing more. I remember the friendliness of an older woman who watched out for me all night. In retrospect, although I felt confident, she saw the child in this seventeen-year-old boy. An onlooker that night would have seen a skinny, drunken boy hanging out with toughened, aging prostitutes, but I experienced beauty.

Similarly, there were days in Ibiza when we would find a quiet spot to swim in the sea; the friends, the company, and the setting made for beautiful times. I remember playing a singing game in my garden with the family. There was so much beauty—not in the voices but in the fun! Or sitting in a boat on a Scottish loch watching my youngest son row toward us on a kayak: That was beauty.

It's not always in the spectacular; I see beauty in the broken and in tragedy. I watched a baptism in a prison. It was the most beautiful meeting I have ever been to. I have knelt in streets with people covered in blood and vomit and seen beauty. I heard a mother give a eulogy at her son's funeral: She said, "I was there when he took his first breath, and I was there when he took his last." That was beautiful—not happy, but beautiful.

We need to stop, see the beauty, and wonder.

Noticing

Have you ever been driving in the car and noticed a glorious sunset reflected in your rearview mirror? Haven't you just wanted to stop the car and look before it fades away into the distance? Life can get a bit like that, where we're so fixed on the next destination that we forget to enjoy the journey. I wonder if sometimes, as earnest Christians, we forget to walk for pleasure. There's always somewhere to be or something to think about.

Genesis 28 tells the story of Jacob. At this point his life had become complex. He had cheated his brother, Esau, out of his inheritance by manipulating and deceiving their father. Esau was understandably angry—actually ready to kill him—so it seemed like a good time to get out of his way. Per his mother's advice, Jacob agreed to leave the area while the dust settled; his father advised him to go to his relatives in Harran and find a wife there. We read:

> Jacob left Beersheba and set out for Harran. When he reached a certain place, he stopped for the night because the sun had set. Taking one of the stones there, he put it under his head and lay down to sleep. He had a dream in which he saw a stairway resting on the earth, with its top reaching to heaven, and the angels of God were ascending and descending on it. There above it stood the LORD, and he said: "I am the LORD, the God of your father Abraham and the God of Isaac. I will give you and your descendants the land on which you are lying. Your descendants will be like the dust of the earth, and you will spread out to the west and to the east, to the north and to the south. All peoples on earth will be blessed through you and your offspring. I am with you and will watch over you wherever you go, and I will bring you back to this land. I will not leave you until I have done what I have promised you."
>
> When Jacob awoke from his sleep, he thought, "Surely the LORD is in this place, and I was not aware of it." He was afraid and said, "How awesome

is this place! This is none other than the house of
God; this is the gate of heaven."

GENESIS 28:10-17

"Surely the LORD is in this place, and I was not aware of
it." I would hate for that to happen to me—to look back over
my days, my months, or even my years and think that surely
God was in this place and I was unaware of it. We need to
increase our God awareness.

According to theologian Derek Kidner, Jacob's response
"expressed profound awe . . . a preoccupation first of all with
the One who had been encountered, not with the things
that were promised."[2] The passage says that Jacob went to
a certain place—nothing special, just a place to rest with a
stone for a pillow, a random spot in the desert. Once Jacob
became aware that God was there, however, it was no longer
just "a certain place": It became an awesome place, and he
expressed profound awe—he worshiped. There's something
about encountering the presence of God that makes everything else secondary.

Noticing leads to wonder; wonder leads to worship. Here
are three tips that help us to notice, to give our attention to
God and live a life of wonder.

Look Back

A helpful exercise is reflecting—looking back and con-
sciously taking note of where you've seen God. It might help
to read back through your journal and identify where God

has been. Can you see him in your reflection? I also think it is helpful at the end of the day to ask yourself where you saw God throughout the day. As you become more attuned to noticing, you really start to stand back in awe and wonder. Looking back helps us notice God in what has passed, but it also trains us to notice him in the present.

A few years ago, my wife and I sat with her grandmother as she lay in her hospital bed. She was in her nineties, had broken her hip, and was feeling sad. But as we chatted, she started to recall her favorite vacation with her husband in Capri, Italy, back in the 1950s. She spoke of walking down to the port, sitting under a lemon tree, enjoying the warmth of the sun, and watching the world go by; as she described the smell of the fragrant lemons, she closed her eyes, breathed in, and smiled. For a moment it felt like she was back there. This long-held memory stirred contentment despite her situation; her smile was a beautiful contrast to the sad face that had greeted us on arrival.

Look Up

At some point during your day today, stop and look up. In Dostoevsky's epic novel *The Brothers Karamazov*, Alyosha looks at the stars above—soft, shining, vast, and fathomless. He becomes very aware of the earth, the dirt beneath his feet, so much so that his wonder leads him to throw himself down on the ground: "He did not know why he was embracing it, he did not try to understand why he longed so irresistibly to kiss it, to kiss all of it."[3] He was moved by wonder. He noticed, he took time, he stopped and allowed himself to be impacted by the beauty of the ordinary dirt and soil in contrast to the vastness of the sky. Go for a walk, peer out your window, stop and look around, try to notice God. You may not end up throwing yourself on the dirt, but I hope you will think of God and your consciousness will be drawn to him.

Look Forward

As Christians, we live with confidence that one day the Kingdom will truly come, the world will be made new, and at the name of Jesus, every knee will bow! We have something to look forward to; he has placed eternity in our hearts, and we live like children anticipating Christmas, the arrival of a King and his Kingdom. If at times we look back and feel pain, or look up and see clouds, we can always look forward and see hope. We don't ignore our present suffering but live as people of hope. A quiet time with the Lord, delving into his Scripture, should make us people of hope, people who look forward. Keith Fournier puts it beautifully: "There really *is* a Divine design. Every morning invites us to begin again. The very structure of the twenty-four-hour cycle of each day reveals the goodness of a God who always invites us—and empowers us—to begin again. Hope is reborn with every sunrise."[4] And, as Paul put it, "May the God of hope fill you with all joy and peace as you trust in him, so that you may overflow with hope by the power of the Holy Spirit" (Romans 15:13).

96

Give Thanks

Living in a culture of consumerism can lead to us to become restless and even unhappy; we need to cultivate a culture of gratitude. Paul encourages us to "give thanks in all circumstances; for this is God's will for you in Christ Jesus" (1 Thessalonians 5:18). We will break the hold of our consumeristic culture when we cultivate gratitude, giving thanks in all circumstances. Consumerism pushes us to focus on what we don't have; a lifestyle of gratitude makes us thankful for what we do have. There is an ancient refrain found repeatedly in the Old Testament: "Give thanks to the LORD, for he is good; his love endures forever." It's one that we would do well to remember and repeat often.

Although what we see can inspire awe and wonder, worship leader Graham Kendrick reminds us that "worship has been misunderstood as something that arises from a feeling which 'comes upon you,' but it is vital that we understand that it is rooted in a conscious act of the will."[5] I like that worship is a "conscious act of the will," a choice we make. The Bible, especially Psalms, is full of references to expressing our worship to God through music and song. Whether you sing to God in the shower at the top of your voice, quietly kneel before him in reverent awe, or do something in between, make it a conscious act of the will to worship him. Author and church leader Francis Chan says, "Isn't it a comfort to worship a God we cannot exaggerate?"[6] I love that when we worship God, we cannot blow him out of proportion; it is impossible to find superlatives and hyperbole for the Author of our faith. I have been disturbed on more than one occasion by someone saying, after a time of worship in a church service, "I didn't get much out of the worship today." My honest response is *Good; we weren't worshiping you.*

The apostle Paul urges, "Do not conform to the pattern of this world" (Romans 12:2). A pattern of consumerism has drifted into our attitude toward many things, including worship—especially sung worship. I recognize that sometimes I think, *I feel low; I'm going to worship because that will make me feel better.* But I've skipped the bit in the middle, which is that when I draw near to God, he draws near to me, his presence lifts me, the words I sing remind me how amazing he is and what a privilege it is to know him, and I do feel better. But the heart of it must be for God, not for me. And part of worship is living in wonder. As 24–7 Prayer cofounder Pete Greig has said, no one has ever stood looking at the northern lights and said, "Wow—aren't I great?"

I really love these words written by G. K. Chesterton; they remind me to remain childlike in my gratitude and worship:

A child kicks his legs rhythmically through
excess, not absence, of life. Because children have
abounding vitality, because they are in spirit fierce
and free, therefore they want things repeated and
unchanged. They always say, "Do it again"; and the
grown-up person does it again until he is nearly

dead. For grown-up people are not strong enough
to exult in monotony. But perhaps God is strong
enough to exult in monotony. It is possible that God
says every morning, "Do it again" to the sun; and
every evening, "Do it again" to the moon. It may not
be automatic necessity that makes all daisies alike; it
may be that God makes every daisy separately, but
has never got tired of making them. It may be that
He has the eternal appetite of infancy; for we have
sinned and grown old, and our Father is younger
than we.[7]

Exult in monotony! That's how to live a life of wonder.

Summary

Life is full of bumps; some big, some small, some we saw
coming and could have avoided, some that were a complete
shock. If as a result we feel we have lost any sense of wonder, we need to realign. As we give our attention to God,
to noticing him in the ordinary as well as the spectacular,
to reflecting and to giving thanks, we will develop a greater
understanding of his majesty, of his lordship, of his power,
of his love, and of his presence.

Here are a few questions to help you think about the role
of wonder in your life:

- *How would I describe my pace lately? Am I go-go-go, or do
  I stop to look up and notice God around me?*

- *When was the last time I stopped and noticed the beauty in something ordinary? What was it that captured me?*

- *Thinking back over the last month, where could I especially see God? Where did I see God in creation? Where did I see God in another person?*

- *What practices of thankfulness do I have in my quiet time?*

- *How do I best express worship that is authentic and God centered?*

8

Persevering

WHEN WE LIVED IN IBIZA, we used to give out copies of the New Testament and Psalms in *The Message* version to people who didn't know Jesus. The title of the book we used was *Jesus Loves Ibiza*, and a friend had designed a striking front cover that I thought perfectly captured the Ibiza vibe. People loved these little Bible portions. We didn't hand them out randomly, as if they were just more flyers for your everyday club night; we mostly gave them as gifts after the sorts of conversations that made such a thing seem appropriate, and we always tried to bookmark a passage that we felt was particularly suitable to the individual we were giving it to. The 24–7 Prayer team in Ibiza continues to do this every summer. Over the years, we had discovered that people loved it when we prayed with them and that they valued the practical help and care we gave those who were in trouble (often due to overindulgence in drinking or drugs). When we first arranged for these portions to be printed, we truly felt that this was a God-inspired idea. But then we started to wonder whether Bibles were something people really wanted or just one more souvenir to take home. We had bought five thousand copies, though, so we persevered. At this time, I found myself leaning very heavily on the verses in Isaiah I referred to earlier:

As the rain and the snow
  come down from heaven,
and do not return to it
  without watering the earth
and making it bud and flourish,
  so that it yields seed for the sower and bread
    for the eater,
so is my word that goes out from my mouth:
  It will not return to me empty,
but will accomplish what I desire
  and achieve the purpose for which I sent it.

ISAIAH 55:10-11

We persevered, believing that we were doing our part in sowing the Word of God; our continual prayer was that as we "sowed" these Bible portions, the Word of God would make an impact—that it would not return empty.

We first started to give away these Bible portions in 2009. Ten years later, in spring 2019, I was at the Big Church Day Out, a festival in the UK where thousands gather and listen to some great Christian bands. I always find it super exciting and faith building. One evening, I managed to find a great spot in the huge crowd; in a lull between sets, I started chatting to the guy next to me, whom I had not met before. I asked where he'd come from; he told me he had come from up north and was helping out with some work at the festival. He went on to explain that he was a recovering addict who had found Jesus. I said that that was amazing and asked him what had led to him Christ. He began, "I was in Ibiza in 2009, and a girl gave me a Bible . . ." He stopped and looked at me. "Why are you crying?"

I explained my tears. It was one of the most beautiful moments of my life. He gave me a great big hug, and we prayed together right in the middle of that field. Somehow God had manufactured a situation that had placed me, in a crowd of twenty-five thousand people, next to a guy whose journey of salvation had begun ten years ago when someone had given him one of our Bible portions in Ibiza! This brief encounter felt like a wonderful gift from the Lord. This man's story of salvation would have been beautiful whether or not I had ever heard it, but God making sure that I did hear it was a big encouragement to me, a vindication for my perseverance.

If Chesterton says that we should exult in monotony and notice the beauty in the ordinary, there is also something beautiful about the monotony of perseverance!

I am hardly going to convince you to go on this journey into a quiet time if I tell you that it will sometimes feel monotonous, that some days it will feel repetitive, that you'll wonder if anything is changing, and that you will just have to get up morning after morning and do it again! But it's true. You won't always see the results of your prayers or your actions quickly—in fact, sometimes not ever. But regardless of whether there are visible results, we are going to have to learn to persevere.

Perseverance in a Culture of Immediacy

One night in Spain, we had been praying for the people who worked and partied on the streets where we worked. One of the volunteers who had joined us on a two-week prayer and mission team said, "It's really boring to pray the same prayer every night." We were taken aback; she had only been with us for eight days, and we had been there, praying the same prayers, for five years. Were we crazy? We didn't get self-righteous or angry, but her words highlighted to us that we live in a culture of immediacy, one in which responses and reactions are quick. Such a culture is not good with perseverance. Romans 12:2 instructs us: "Do not conform to the pattern of this world, but be transformed by the renewing of your mind. Then you will be able to test and approve what God's will is—his good, pleasing and perfect will." If we are called to live counterculturally, not conforming to the patterns of this world, we must understand that one of the drivers of our culture, particularly in the Western world, is immediacy.

If photos don't load quickly on my laptop, I get frustrated; if a movie starts to buffer while I am watching it, I want to change internet providers; if my fast-food order takes five minutes to arrive at the counter, I become hangry! I message a friend in Malaysia, and she replies in seconds; I want a new T-shirt and can buy it instantly, fully expecting to be able to wear it the next day; I can pay my bills in seconds, run up a huge debt in a day, and borrow more to cover it by evening. I can order an Uber in moments to travel into the city or book a flight to New York and be there by morning. We live in an instant world. If we want it and can find a way to pay for it, we can get it—and we can get it quickly. For our generation to survive and thrive, we need to learn the art of perseverance in a culture of immediacy, which may not come without deliberate effort.

We can't be conformed to the pattern of immediacy in our prayer times—it's just not how God works! I am not saying that I don't believe that God can do things instantly and immediately; most of the time when I pray, I am asking and hoping for his immediate intervention, so please never stop praying that way. Still, God doesn't answer our prayers like a genie in a bottle or a fairy godmother offering us three wishes. He is not a divine vending machine. Jesus told his disciples that they should ask and keep asking, seek and keep seeking, knock and keep knocking (Matthew 7:7).

I love the Old Testament story of the children of Israel escaping from Egypt. Following a series of dramatic, God-instigated events, they finally leave the country and their enforced slavery there with the hope of a better future ahead. The Egyptians pursue them, intent on recapturing them and returning them to slavery. They close in on the children of Israel just as they have reached the Red Sea. With the Egyptians behind them and the sea in front of them, with no boats to take them across, there is seemingly no way forward for the Israelites. All they can see is impending disaster. Yet the moment that looks like their greatest crisis as a nation will become the very day on which "the LORD saved Israel from the hands of the Egyptians" (Exodus 14:30). The miracle happens. It may look immediate, but they've experienced four hundred years of travail, sorrow, pain, and perseverance before, in just one moment, Moses raises his staff, the sea miraculously parts, and they walk over the dry seabed to freedom. Irish biblical scholar J. Alec Moyter comments on this story: "Let us learn the lesson: it is the will of God that gives purpose to life. There is always the 'bigger picture' of which he is aware and we are not."[1] Perseverance is about recognizing that we are part of a bigger picture; there is often much more at play than we realize, and sometime we don't see instant results.

One Person's *Suddenly* Is Another Person's *Constantly*
The apostle Paul prayed for people constantly, and in his constant praying, things suddenly happened! We read of this in Romans 1:8-10 (emphasis mine):

> First, I thank my God through Jesus Christ for all of you, because your faith is being reported all over the

world. God, whom I serve in my spirit in preaching the gospel of his Son, is my witness how *constantly* I remember you in my prayers at all times; and I pray that now at last by God's will the way may be opened for me to come to you.

And again in 2 Thessalonians 1:11:

With this in mind, we *constantly* pray for you, that our God may make you worthy of his calling, and that by his power he may bring to fruition your every desire for goodness and your every deed prompted by faith.

Once more, in 2 Timothy 1:3:

I thank God, whom I serve, as my ancestors did, with a clear conscience, as night and day I *constantly* remember you in my prayers.

The emphasis is my own, but Paul's frequent repetition of the word *constantly* clearly tells us something.

My dad prays for people constantly; he gets up early to do it every day. When my mother died back in 1981, my three brothers and I all handled it differently. I think they all coped much better than I did at the time. I made a complete mess of grieving. It took me nine years to find a healthy place with my pain, my grief, and God. Although at the time one of my brothers had seemed to handle the same emotions in a less destructive way than I did, he later went on a long journey of grief, mental illness, divorce, and pain. He tried his best and was a real help and example to me as someone who just kept going and coping with the various circumstances of life as he grew up, but he didn't arrive at a comfortable place with his faith until 2011.

At that time, I said to my dad, "Isn't it amazing that he has come back to the Lord?"

My dad gently responded, "I pray for him every day—I've done that for all of you all your lives."

Then it dawned on me; he had prayed for me when I'd been expelled from school, when I'd started drinking and taking drugs, when I'd been homeless, when I'd been in prison. Over those five years, the changes he saw had looked worse, not better. He had prayed for my other brother for thirty years and seen no apparent change; then one day his *constantly* became my *suddenly*; his *constantly* became my brother's *suddenly*.

This journey has to be one of constantly saying, *I will not let go until you do something, Lord. I will keep giving out Bibles even if I don't see the results. I will keep offering up prayers, year in, year out, even when I see no noticeable change.* Thirty years into this ride as a Christian, I realize that constant perseverance is essential. I love the instant—I have seen the instant— but it's the constant that remains necessary.

We need to learn such perseverance in an immediate culture.

Quantity Leads to Quality

All parents want quality time with their children, and I am entirely in favor of planning special days together. I love significant moments with my boys—conversations and times we can look back on fondly, memories that make our relationships stronger. But I have learned that it is hard to schedule quality time. Children are not always in the right frame of mind: Sometimes they are tired, or they have schoolwork that needs doing, or they want to hang out with their friends. This is what I have discovered: Put in the quantity time, and the quality time will happen.

I spent a lot of time with my boys as they were growing up. I drove them to school most mornings; I hung out with them, playing *Call of Duty* until I became reasonably good for an old guy; I walked the dog with them; we went on vacations together. Most of the quality moments, the real "golden memory" moments, have come out of ordinary quantity time. The unexpected conversations—the spontaneous moments of sharing dreams, worries, hopes, and fears—don't always wait for a planned family evening; they can emerge over a Tuesday evening drying the dishes. In the midst of quantity time, we have quality moments.

I think quiet time works in a similar way. Imagine if there were a chapter in the book of Acts, say three hundred verses long, that said something like "And Paul got up, made a tent, and then went to bed" or "Peter went fishing. The sea was calm; he caught enough fish for his family. Then he went home, cooked the fish, and slept." Hundreds of New

Testament days must have been like this—the apostles doing their normal, everyday thing: maybe praying, pondering, journaling a little, meditating on the words of Jesus; loads of repetitive perseverance. But occasionally, the magic would happen!

I wrote a book about our time in Ibiza, and of course I mostly focused on the best bits. But I could have written a whole chapter that was "I got up, ate breakfast, walked the dog, went to the gym, prayed, read my Bible, collected the kids from school, watched a movie, and then went to bed." We tend to look at people's highlight reels. The book of Acts is a highlight reel. We all try to communicate in a way that is engaging and inspiring, but we have to remember that, in practice, not every moment of our lives is exciting, including our quiet times. You know that there will be days when it will feel dull and monotonous, but if you keep doing it, you will have quality moments. Beware of a spirituality that is all about the highs; enjoy them when they come, but when they don't, remember that God hasn't gone anywhere, and persevere.

Perseverance Requires Repetition

A while ago, I realized that I needed to build this kind of persevering rhythm into my quiet time. There were a whole bunch of people I wanted to pray for regularly: family, friends, and other people I have met. When I say "I will pray for you," I don't want it to be well intentioned in the moment but unfulfilled in practice. I sincerely want to do it. When I meet someone who says "I've been praying for you," I want it to be more than a quick "God bless Brian" when they saw me heading in their direction. Recognizing my own weakness in this, I decided that I must find a way for my good intentions to be positive actions. So I started a list of people I would pray for every week.

My list looks quite battered now. I'm still using the same piece of paper after several years. It started as quite a short list of about thirty neatly written and nicely spaced names. But the list has grown now to 375 names that are much more squashed together, and I fear it might just keep growing! Perhaps you will find the same if you begin to cultivate your own list. Don't be afraid to start small and watch it grow. It takes me more than an hour a week to sit down and pray briefly yet sincerely for each person on my list, but I am determined to persevere in prayer for various people around the world I know and love. I have constructed a prayer or a few words that are written down for each couple, family, or individual so that when I arrive at them on my list, I already know what to pray. When I'm aware of something that is currently important for them, I pray about that, too. For some, I have a specific Bible verse I pray for them. I've found that this helps me focus and keep to my commitment to pray. In this designated time, I keep my phone within reach so that if I think I should share a Bible verse or some encouragement with someone I'm praying for, I can do it there and then. Sometimes my message might be as simple as "I'm praying for you today." Here are a few of the prayers I have written down for people:

Lord, be with x and y—may they encounter you and also find strength, grace, and friends.

Lead a and b—may they know joy and grow in leadership.

Be with j—give him his heart's desire and provide for him.

These handwritten words remind me how to pray for the people on my list, but there are many different ways you can do this. One of my friends has photos of the people he's praying for that pop up every day on his iPad to remind him. You could use a to-do list or set of calendar reminders on your phone. At 24–7 Prayer, we have developed the Inner Room app, which helps you build a list so that you can easily practice regular perseverance and intercession for people.

Persevering in Prayer for Bigger Things

This kind of persistent, regular prayer is also good for your neighborhood, for your town or city, for your church, for the people you work with, for your government, for your nation, and for your generation. It's also good to pray for other churches and other nations.

These verses from Isaiah 62:6-7 are beautiful and worth memorizing to inspire us to persist in prayer:

I have posted watchmen on your walls, Jerusalem;
    they will never be silent day or night.
You who call on the LORD,
    give yourselves no rest,

and give him no rest till he establishes Jerusalem
and makes her the praise of the earth.

During our time in Ibiza, we used to go to the same spot regularly and pray the whole chapter of Isaiah 62 over the town of San Antonio. The location was right next to an ancient watchtower with a view over the town, which added a little extra poignancy. Try finding your own spot to go and regularly pray over a specific area. (A watchtower is a beautiful but nonessential extra!) Find a verse to regularly pray over a specific situation, nation, or town. Bible commentator Albert Barnes paraphrases these verses: "Keep not silence yourselves, nor let him rest in silence. Pray without ceasing; and do not intermit your efforts until the desires of your hearts shall be granted, and Zion shall be established and the world saved."[2] We don't let God rest in silence, as we pray without ceasing. Throughout the Bible, God exhorts us through his prophets and teachers to be people who persevere and pray. He looks for this; he expects it.

Summary

Learning perseverance in a culture of immediacy will take training and practice. It takes faith to pray constantly, with the hope that one day the answer will come suddenly. And it will only be through investing quantity time in prayer that we have those quality moments of breakthrough. Here are some practical points that I hope will help:

- Write a list of things you have been praying for consistently. How is God meeting you in this?

- Write a list of names of others you would love to come to know Jesus. What simple prayer can you pray for them today?

- Start a list of other people you will commit to pray for regularly, and determine how often you will pray for them.

- Consider writing short prayers for the people on your list to help you pray consistently.

- Challenge yourself to send at least one encouraging message or Bible verse to someone on your list every time you pray.

- If you're praying for your town, find a place you can go that will inspire you as you pray.

- Why not download the 24–7 Prayer Inner Room app? This is a fantastic tool for helping you order your prayer life and compile digital lists.

9

Simplicity

A NUMBER OF YEARS AGO, we had the opportunity to rent a farmhouse, a beautiful, nine-hundred-year-old building set in vast grounds on top of a hill in Ibiza. The house was surrounded by sunny terraces from which you could gaze on the olive, fig, pomegranate, almond, and lemon trees and the Mediterranean Sea beyond. The house itself was old and quirky, with open fireplaces, steep staircases, rooms that opened into other rooms, and doorways that you had to duck to pass through. The kitchen even had an ancient bread oven built into the walls. We moved there with two other people and thought it was going to be idyllic. We had visions of bringing workers to our home in the summer to escape the noise and busyness of San Antonio for refreshment; of creating a retreat center; of the land itself being a place where people could come and feel healed and restored. The house itself was quite basic, but we were all excited—simplicity beckoned.

We very quickly learned one thing: Living simply is *complex.*

Within three weeks, we had run out of water. What we'd thought was a well that would provide the house with all our water needs turned out to be just a cistern that relied on rainwater—and there wasn't a lot of that in southern Spain! Instead, we had to pay for a truck to transport water up the hill and fill the cistern. It was expensive, and we became very conscious of water usage. Showers took on a whole new level of complexity: Fill a bucket with the first rush of cold water to use for flushing the toilet later, switch off the water while lathering up with shower gel or rubbing shampoo into your hair, and certainly do not linger to just enjoy the feel of cool water in the summer or hot water on winter mornings.

The walls of the ancient house were two feet thick, designed to keep cool in summer and hold the heat in winter, which sounds sensible. But nine hundred years ago, no thought had been given to the need for mobile phone reception or an internet signal, and the remote location meant that, despite the assurances given before we moved in, no telephone company would connect a landline to facilitate a broadband connection. We had to install an expensive satellite phone system with limited bandwidth for seven people, two of whom were teenagers and "needed" their Xbox connection! Living overseas, the rest of us struggled with the disconnection from friends and family back home, especially because video calls became impossible.

To top it all off, we were powered by solar electricity. We had loved that idea—on such a sunny island, it seemed like a no-brainer. But the system was old and had faults in its installation, which meant that once the solar power's stored-in batteries ran out, a diesel generator would kick in—and of course the generator needed fuel. One use of the washing machine on a cloudy day meant that the whole house would lose electricity.

We felt isolated, drained, and frustrated. It crept into our relationships, pushing us all to the breaking point. At first, we soldiered on, and I wish I could finish this paragraph by saying that we triumphed and the simple life became our way of life. But we didn't; it beat us. We were running a busy, successful ministry, but adding the "simple life" had been too much. So, after ten months, we left the farmhouse, came down the hill, and returned to more typical twenty-first-century accommodation. Living simply wasn't easy.

Something that helped me understand this time, and what had gone wrong, was this insight from Richard Foster: "The Christian Discipline of simplicity is an *inward* reality that results in an *outward* life-style."[1] We had gone for an outward lifestyle without truly understanding the inward reality of simplicity. Idealism can blur reality, but I still believe in simplicity. Matthew 6:16-34 gives helpful teaching on how to live simply in a complex world: Jesus talks about the practice of fasting, understanding what we treasure, and addressing anxiety.

Fasting

> "When you fast, do not look somber as the hypocrites do, for they disfigure their faces to show others they are fasting. Truly I tell you, they have received their reward in full. But when you fast, put oil on your head and wash your face, so that it will not be obvious to others that you are fasting, but only to your Father, who is unseen; and your Father, who sees what is done in secret, will reward you."
>
> MATTHEW 6:16-18

So what is fasting? American author Dallas Willard refers to fasting as something that "confirms our utter dependence upon God by finding in him a source of sustenance beyond food."[2] There is something deeply authentic about a fasting Christian, someone who is willing to go to the Father and say, "I need you more than food." Fasting is about going without food for spiritual purposes. The Bible is full of people who fasted: Moses, the lawgiver; Hannah, the mother of Samuel; David, the shepherd-king; Elijah, the prophet; Esther, the queen; Anna, the prophetess—right through to Jesus and on to the apostles and members of the early church. Modern missionaries like Amy Carmichael, Mother Teresa, and Jackie Pullinger all fasted. You could read a whole book on fasting, and one I think is helpful is an old classic: *God's Chosen Fast* by Arthur Wallis.

The discipline of fasting will hone your quiet times, draw you much closer to the Lord, enable helpful self-examination, and sharpen your intercessory prayer life. But fasting is so much more than a "What do I get out of it?" discipline. We can overly focus on developing personal gifts, spiritual gifts, healing, and specific answers to prayer, but as John Wesley said about fasting, "First, let it be done unto the Lord, with our eye singly fixed on him."[3] We don't fast to get; fasting does not twist God's arm. Fasting indicates our hunger and seriousness for God and his Kingdom. It is not some spiritual exercise whereby we lose weight. Indeed, a professor once told me that well-meaning Christians who have an eating disorder can sometimes "attach themselves to fasting, telling themselves they are being great Christians doing a spiritual discipline—which it is, of course—but really just be spiritualizing their disorder." Fasting does not have to do with physical weight. Rather, it reveals to us whether we are carrying unhelpful, or even sinful, weight in our spiritual walk.

Fasting will highlight your desires, both good ones and dark ones. As your physical hunger is accentuated, you may find other desires accentuated, such as lust, anger, greed, and selfishness. You will discover what you turn to when you are tired or hungry. Refusing to give in to the urges of hunger strengthens us when it comes to resisting other kinds of temptation—or, as summarized by Thomas à Kempis: "Refrain from gluttony and thou shalt the more easily restrain all the inclinations of the flesh."[4] Cutting out meals also gives you more time to focus on prayer. If it's possible within your family life, use the time when you would be eating or preparing food to pray.

Note that Jesus said, "when you fast." There was an expectation that followers of Jesus would observe this practice. But we would do well to remember that even with this expectation it is an invitation, not a command.

If fasting is new to you or the very idea of it sounds daunting, start with a twelve-hour fast; eat nothing from the time you get up until your evening meal. This was common practice in Jesus' time, something people often did twice a week. (Again, I'm not talking about following the trend of intermittent fasting for weight loss; this ought to be done "unto the Lord.") From there, you could go for a twenty-four-hour fast. We've found that the best way to start is to skip your evening meal and then miss breakfast and lunch the next day; some people still prefer to go one whole day without eating at all.

I'd really encourage you to build a regular twelve-hour or twenty-four-hour practice of fasting into your life. I would recommend telling a trusted friend for support or fasting with somebody. (This is very different from trying to let everyone know, something Jesus criticized.) And remember, it's a food fast—keep your fluids up! As you grow in this, you may want to fast for a longer period—three days, five days, a week. Some have fasted for twenty-one days, a month, or even pushed it to the outer limits of the forty-day fast, as

Jesus did, but you should not attempt this without first reading thoroughly on the subject to understand the physical and spiritual aspects of what you are undertaking.

Although we sometimes hear people talk about fasting from a specific thing, that is not fasting—it's abstaining. Abstaining is about discipline and control, often an expression of the thoughts *This has become too dominant in my life* or *I am distracted by this* or *I do this too much*, which lead us to identifying what it is we treasure.

Treasures in Heaven

"Do not store up for yourselves treasures on earth,
where moths and vermin destroy, and where thieves
break in and steal. But store up for yourselves treasures
in heaven, where moths and vermin do not destroy,
and where thieves do not break in and steal. For where
your treasure is, there your heart will be also."

MATTHEW 6:19-21

At some point in your quiet time, it is helpful to ask yourself the question *What do I treasure?* In practical terms: *What do I spend my money on? What do I give my time to? What do my thoughts dwell on?* Questions like these help us discern what we value, and what we value is what we treasure.

What we treasure reveals a lot about ourselves, our priorities, our loves, our desires. I treasure family, marriage, friendship, church, holidays—and a lot of these are good, maybe even heavenly, treasures. But there are other things that I give my time and energy to that demonstrate that they are also treasures to me—things that I'm less happy to admit to and am pretty sure are not heavenly.

One way to test whether these things are "treasures" is to ask ourselves, *Could I give it up or give it away?* Removing some of the unhelpful or even destructive clutter that we hold on to is a great step toward simplicity. Abstaining from something for a while really highlights how much we value it and whether we are relying on it more than on God. Have we buried God under the weight of all our treasures?

Do Not Worry

"Therefore I tell you, do not worry about your life, what you will eat or drink; or about your body, what you will wear. Is not life more than food, and the body more than clothes? Look at the birds of the air; they do not sow or reap or store away in barns, and yet your heavenly Father feeds them. Are you not much more valuable than they? Can any one of you by worrying add a single hour to your life?

"And why do you worry about clothes? See how the flowers of the field grow. They do not labor or spin. Yet I tell you that not even Solomon in all his splendor was dressed like one of these. If that is how God clothes the grass of the field, which is here today and tomorrow is thrown into the fire, will he

not much more clothe you—you of little faith? So
do not worry, saying, 'What shall we eat?' or 'What
shall we drink?' or 'What shall we wear?' For the
pagans run after all these things, and your heavenly
Father knows that you need them. But seek first his
kingdom and his righteousness, and all these things
will be given to you as well. Therefore do not worry
about tomorrow, for tomorrow will worry about
itself. Each day has enough trouble of its own."

MATTHEW 6:25-34

It only takes a simple Google search to discover that anxiety
is a huge problem in our society today. There are things that
happen to us and circumstances that we find ourselves in
that are out of our control, incredibly challenging, and very
distressing. These can cause us to worry, and the last thing
we need in those moments is someone coming up to us and
saying, "Just don't worry about it." What does help is praying
(bringing our concerns to Jesus and asking for his peace in
the situation, trusting that our heavenly Father knows what
we need); asking friends and people in our church community to pray with us and support us; and, of course, taking
professional advice when that is appropriate.

We worry about lots of other things, too, that have more
to do with the growing complexity of the times we live in.
There is evidence that supports the idea that simplicity—
decluttering, uncomplicating, and simplifying our lives both
physically and mentally—reduces anxiety.

If simplicity is the opposite of complexity, I can understand how this works. In our Western society, we have so many choices, and most of the time we consider that to be a good thing. But it comes with its downside. When we have a choice or even many options, we worry about making the wrong choice. I once visited a restaurant that had just one dish on the menu—it was liberating!

Years ago, there was a sense that when you came home, you shut the door and left the outside world behind. That doesn't happen anymore—the internet has changed our relationship to spatial boundaries, and someone can post a critical comment about me when I am relaxing in my bed at the end of the day. I don't see this complexity waning just yet, so we have to simplify the menu and work out how to shut the door.

Whether our worries are about things outside our control or can be mitigated by simplifying our lives, Paul gives us this beautiful invitation:

> Do not be anxious about anything, but in every
> situation, by prayer and petition, with thanksgiving,
> present your requests to God. And the peace of God,
> which transcends all understanding, will guard your
> hearts and your minds in Christ Jesus.
>
> PHILIPPIANS 4:6-7

As we go back to our quiet time, we create time and space that allows God to visit us with his peace that "transcends all understanding." It's here that we bring our anxieties to him, talk with him about the choices we face, speak about the things that intrude on our peace. It's interesting that Paul talks about anxiety in Philippians 4:6-7, but in the space of just five more verses, he goes on to talk about being content: "I have learned to be content, whatever the circumstances" (PHILLIPS). It seems to me that not being anxious is closely linked to being content, not fretting about what we do or do not have.

Summary
Fasting, identifying, and decluttering unhelpful treasure, and bringing our complex worries to God can help us live more simply. Here are some questions that will help you get started. As you consider them, remember Paul's words in Philippians 4:6-7.

1. *Fasting.* Look back at the ways to get started with fasting. Make a plan!
   - *When will I next fast, and for how long?*
   - *Is there somebody I would like to join me on the fast?*
   - *Can I establish a regular routine of fasting? What would that look like?*

2. *Treasure.* Carry out a little evaluation by asking yourself these questions:
   - *What do I spend my money on?*
   - *What do I give my time to?*

- *What do my thoughts dwell on?*
- *Which of those things do I need to give up or give away?*

3. *Worry.* Simplify the menu and shut the door.
   - *What choices or forthcoming decisions are making me anxious right now?* Allocate an amount of time to spend praying about them in your quiet time, and ask someone else to pray about them too.
   - *What things have been said to me—digitally or verbally—that are causing me anxiety?* (Again, pray about these, and ask someone else to pray too.)
   - *What times of day would it be helpful for me to put all devices away?*

10

Hidden Life

ELIJAH IS ONE OF MY FAVORITE people in the Bible. There is a powerful story recounted in 1 Kings 17 that tells of when Elijah first revealed himself to the evil King Ahab. The Bible says that King Ahab "did more to provoke the LORD, the God of Israel, to anger than all the kings of Israel who were before him" (1 Kings 16:33, ESV)—he wasn't a good guy! Elijah shows up from nowhere and informs Ahab that it will not rain for a few years. This is particularly insulting; Baal, Ahab's god, is supposedly a god of rain, and Elijah has just announced that there's not going to be any!

Elijah's introduction is brief; unlike many other people in the Bible, he doesn't even get a genealogy, just the information that he's from the hill country. Yet somehow he ends up in a place of prominence in the king's court, where he proclaims an edict from God that will have a profound impact on the nation: "There shall be neither rain nor dew these years, except by my word" (1 Kings 17:1, ESV). This is a significant word delivered in a prominent place, all contained in just one verse. The next two verses go on to record God saying to Elijah, "Depart from here and turn eastward and hide yourself" (1 Kings 17:3, ESV). Elijah moves very quickly from a place of prominence to a place of hiddenness, and we can learn a lot from him when it comes to quiet times.

Hide Yourself!
In the place of hiddenness, Elijah is the recipient of some very unusual provision from God. Tucked away in a relatively inaccessible place near a small stream, he is fed by ravens every morning and evening. The Old Testament law makes it clear that ravens are considered unclean and Jewish people should go nowhere near them, let alone be fed by them! This was way outside Elijah's comfort zone. This time and space he's inhabiting is a world away from the royal palace; it's a solitary place and a period of utter helplessness in which he is totally reliant on God for nourishment and comfort.

The story goes on to explain that after a while the stream dries up. Sometimes it feels like that happens in our quiet times, too. Elijah leaves his spot by the stream and travels farther, into enemy territory, where he is miraculously provided for by a widow. This presents yet another challenge for

Elijah: He is a grown man, a man of God, asking for help from a widow, who is herself dependent on charity—this is culturally awkward and humbling. Yet in this moment of humility, God acts miraculously: He provides an unlimited supply of flour and oil, which is plenty for both Elijah and the widow's family to live on.

If we feel like the stream has dried up in our quiet times, it may be time to find another place of hiddenness. I don't mean a new chair; I mean a new way. Sometimes God will allow things to happen in your life that make you more dependent on him; he wants to keep moving you to a greater level of dependence, a deeper level of faith. Sometimes to do that he will allow something that was once helpful to dry up. Something I discovered a while ago was that it's easy to get stuck on autopilot when it comes to quiet time! Of course, God doesn't change, and he's always present. But I do think the special ways we connect with him change over the years, so please don't be surprised when it happens. If quiet time feels dry, it might be time to change some aspect of your approach—the time, the place, the manner—but it is never time to stop. God spoke to Elijah in the dryness!

Three years after God first commands Elijah to hide himself, God says to him, "Go, show yourself" (1 Kings 18:1, ESV). Elijah goes back and proclaims that it will now rain.

Imagine how frustrating and terrifying the waiting might have been at times, especially with no idea when the period of waiting would come to an end. Hiddenness probably wasn't easy. But imagine what Elijah learned in the waiting.

During that time, a young boy was raised from the dead, and there was supernatural provision of food through three whole years of drought. Elijah's prophetic proclamation fulfilled by the subsequent lack of rain had led him to a place where the miraculous became his daily experience. He spoke it, and then he lived it. He began by proclaiming the Word; in hiddenness, he learned to live the Word.

In a culture that values prominence, celebrity, recognition, and public affirmation, how well do we cope with the idea of hiddenness?

There is something important about hiddenness and much to be learned in it. Seeds germinate in darkness; a baby develops for nine months hidden in the womb before it is ready to emerge; the Olympic gymnast performing a ninety-second floor exercise spends countless hours practicing in the gym without spectators; the skyscraper sits on a hidden foundation deep underground. I am so glad that when I came back to God from prison, the church I became part of didn't regularly ask me to stand up and tell my story. They allowed me to remain hidden and grow in my faith without the pressure of expectations from others. Telling stories of how God has worked in our lives is great—it encourages the church and inspires them to keep telling others about Jesus—but this was a wise decision at a time when my young ego might have reveled in the attention. I did tell my story eventually, but it was as if my church allowed me to fly under the radar for a while, and that really protected me.

It's mostly below the radar where we learn about God;

where we become dependent on, comforted by, and nourished by him; where we begin to trust that he knows what he is doing; and where the lessons we learn are unique to us. Sometimes we are fed by ravens and looked after by widows. Hiddenness prepares us for the moments when we are visible.

The Pressure to Be Seen

Culturally, we can feel compelled to reveal ourselves, or at least the parts of ourselves we want people to see. We view other people's highlight reels and reveal our own carefully constructed version of who we want to be seen as by others. One of my bigger battles in writing this book is the fact that once you put something down on paper, you are no longer hidden. Plus, if you write a book, you have to promote it, talk about it, sell it—believe me, it's a quandary!

Sometimes it's not so much the pressure of being seen as the desire to be recognized—not necessarily as a form of celebrity but as an acknowledgment of our efforts. Most of us have been in situations where we've put in hours of work and effort and then someone else has taken the credit. We know that God rewards what is done in secret, but we'd like other people to notice as well! It's a challenge to swallow our pride and graciously accept hiddenness.

Hiddenness comes in many guises and is predominantly an internal battle. Some of us find it easier than others. Jesus was relatively hidden for the first thirty years of his life. After the initial account of his birth, he only pops up briefly into our view again at the age of twelve when we read about him engaging in discussion with leaders at the Temple, and then we see nothing again for another eighteen years. Thirty years of hiddenness and three years in view! I'm not a mathematician, but even I can work out that it's only about 10 percent of Jesus' life that is in public view. Thirty years of hiddenness . . . and I can't even cope with a six-week break from social media!

In his three years of ministry, Jesus picked up followers. It makes me chuckle when I read the word *followers* in the Gospels in light of today's culture, where the number of followers you have seems to be increasingly important. Jesus' followers literally followed him around, wanting to hear his teaching and perhaps hoping to be on the receiving end of one of his miracles. Even so, Jesus found times of hiddenness, spending full nights in prayer. We hear snippets of what was said during those times, but there must be much more that we don't know about.

Then things started to shift.

Jesus Lost Followers!

Jesus' teaching became increasingly challenging, and people struggled with what he had to say; it wasn't what they wanted to hear. Jesus started to lose followers. We read that "many of his disciples turned back and no longer *followed* him" (John 6:66, emphasis mine). This leads us to John 7:1-24, which I think could be seen as a reflection on social media.

Jesus was a Jew, and it was obligatory for every male Jew living within a fifteen-mile radius of Jerusalem to go to the

Feast of Booths in Jerusalem, Judea. Jesus' brothers prepared to go and then said to Jesus, "Leave here and go to Judea, that your disciples also may see the works you are doing. For no one works in secret if he seeks to be known openly. If you do these things, show yourself to the world" (John 7:3-4, ESV).

Wow, that is so real for many of us—the constant pressure to show ourselves to the world. Quite possibly, there was pressure on Jesus to revive his support, to regain followers, to position himself as the Messiah, the main man in Jerusalem. Jesus' reply is interesting:

> "You go to the festival. I am not going up to this
> festival, because my time has not yet fully come."
> After he had said this, he stayed in Galilee.
> However, after his brothers had left for the festival,
> he went also, not publicly, but in secret.
> JOHN 7:8-10

What? Did Jesus just lie to his brothers? Actually, the key is in the different uses of the word *time*. If Jesus meant that his final destiny, his God-ordained time, was not yet ready, John would have used the Greek word *hora*, which means "the destined hour of God." But the word used is *kairos*, which means "opportunity" or "the best moment." William Barclay says, "Jesus is saying simply, 'If I go up with you just now I will not get the opportunity I am looking for. The time is not opportune.' . . . Jesus is choosing his time with careful prudence in order to get the most effective results."[1] Timing is important.

The brothers wanted Jesus to go with them on their journey. They wanted to bring him up from under the radar, but he understood timing. They were ready to elevate him, but the time wasn't right. They were getting ahead of him, rushing him. A friend of mine once said, "Nothing slows you down more than trying to get ahead of God." Jesus' brothers were well intentioned but were getting ahead of God, and it was all mixed up with this pressure to go public. But Jesus takes his time, chooses to remain hidden, goes up privately to Jerusalem. And then, in the middle of the feast, when the timing is right, Jesus gets up and begins to teach.

This is a master class in not bowing to pressure. Jesus shows us how to remain hidden. He knew how to hide himself and also how to show himself. Take your time; don't let other people push you out of hiddenness. When Jesus did show himself, he naturally brought to light what he had learned in the quiet place, in the hidden place. People marveled at his astounding authority and ability to teach despite his lack of formal learning.

View your quiet time as the hidden place. In the hidden place, we gain understanding of timing; in the hidden place, we deal with disappointment when it seems like our time hasn't come; in the hidden place, we deal with moments when we've felt overlooked. We learn the joy of hiddenness and embrace the beauty of doing the right thing at the right time.

My wise friend also said, "The only thing harder than waiting on God is wishing you had!" Embrace the times of hiddenness, the times of waiting; find joy in them.

Summary

In a world full of highlight reels and productivity output, it is hard to invest in the hidden. Yet this is precisely what Jesus calls our quiet times to be. As we draw this chapter to a close, you may find it helpful to reflect on the following questions:

- Have a look at your social-media output. Does it represent who you are? Perhaps you can challenge yourself to post a picture of yourself, natural and unfiltered, as a way of owning the unique individual God has made you to be.

- Practice social-media abstinence. Depending on how much you currently use social media, reduce it to a specific time or day or abstain from it completely for a set period of time. Once you've done this: How do you feel? How does it affect your enjoyment of moments without being able to post them? How does it affect your relationship with God, yourself, and others?

11

Generosity

I've started to realize that as I get older I get more like my father. I never wanted this to happen. Not that I don't like my dad; it's just that I've always felt I'm my own man! But I have recognized that the time I spent with my father in my early years has given me some of his characteristics (some good, some bad). To some extent, I am a reflection of Billy Heasley.

In a similar way, the relationship we are developing with God in our quiet times, in the quiet place, will have an impact on how we live our lives. In other words, what happens in the chair shouldn't stay in the chair—it should be visible in how we live. The more time we spend with God, the more we become like him; to some extent, we become a reflection of him.

One of God's characteristics is his generosity. We read in John 3:16, "For God so loved the world that he gave his one and only Son." God gave! He gave his one and only Son. (I find it strange that sometimes the emphasis is on the "one and only Son"; I have two sons, and I don't think that having an extra would make it easy for me to give one of them away!) What an example! I understand the powerful love of the perfect Father because God gave; I enjoy this rich and intimate relationship with Jesus because God gave; I experience the presence and guidance of the Holy Spirit because God gave. Time and time again, I am bowled over by the generosity of God.

This giving of Jesus, as huge a gift as that was, doesn't sit in isolation as the only demonstration of God's generosity. James announces, "Every good and perfect gift is from above, coming down from the Father of the heavenly lights, who does not change like shifting shadows" (James 1:17).

Ownership

We should be generous because God is generous. As we think about being generous ourselves, it's helpful to ask, *Who owns what?*

Way back in the beginning, God said to Adam and Eve, "Be fruitful and multiply and fill the earth and subdue it, and have dominion over the fish of the sea and over the birds of the heavens and over every living thing that moves on the earth" (Genesis 1:28, ESV). In other words: "Look after this; be good stewards of it." Psalm 24 reminds us that the earth is the Lord's, and everything in it. The fundamental principle of stewardship is that God, the creator of this earth, owns everything and has given us a mandate to look after it. Tim Keller makes this überchallenging when he says, "A lack of generosity refuses to acknowledge that your assets are not really yours, but God's."[1] Peter seems to take it even further when he encourages us with this statement: "Each of you should use whatever gift you have received to serve others, as faithful stewards of God's grace in its various forms" (1 Peter 4:10). Not only are we to be faithful stewards, but we are also to use what we have received to serve others—everything that we have received, including money.

Steward is an old-fashioned word that we don't use much these days. Dictionaries define it in different ways, such as these: "a person who manages another's property or financial affairs"; "one who administers anything as the agent of another"; and "a person who has charge of the household of another."[2] It all sounds quite Victorian. What I think it all points to is that we have the responsibility to use the gifts God gives us in a wise and godly way that serves others.

We would do well in our quiet times to regularly ask this type of question: *Am I being a faithful and generous steward of God's money and possessions?* Maybe we don't always do this because we think, *I earned it; I deserve it. It's mine, not God's.* We may not ever say these words, but perhaps there's an inward *amen* to Bart Simpson's memorable thanksgiving prayer: "Dear God, we paid for all this stuff ourselves, so thanks for nothing."[3]

There is freedom that comes with understanding who owns what and our own role as stewards. There is joy for us as stewards in expressing the generous heart of the Father by being generous, just as he is generous.

Thankfulness

We've already talked about thankfulness and how it ought to be a key part of any quiet time. Grateful people tend to be generous people. They seem to have grasped what Jesus meant when he said that it is "more blessed to give than to receive" (Acts 20:35).

During our time overseas, we relied on the generosity of kind people who supported us financially. The work we felt we were called to do wasn't paid, but it took too many hours of our time to be able to take other paid work that would cover our living costs. Some gave a regular monthly amount; other support was sent randomly or came as one-off gifts. After several years in the UK when money had been tight, my wife and I had finally arrived at a stage where we both had reasonably well-paying jobs and felt fairly confident in our financial self-sufficiency. So it was a challenge not only to relinquish that to move to Spain but also to realize when we looked at the numbers that the amount of guaranteed monthly support, while wonderful, was still not enough to cover the monthly bills and food.

Maybe it sounds naïve, but we felt assurance that God

would provide. We had an attitude that was simply this: *God, if you want us there, we trust that you'll give us enough to pay the bills, to eat, and to provide for our children.* After all, we had read God's promise to "meet all your needs according to my glorious riches in Christ Jesus" (Philippians 4:19, PAR). We had noted that it didn't say "all your wants," but we were happy enough with our needs! This quickly became one of our verses for the occasional storms of doubt and wavering faith that blew in around our finances.

Initially, our quiet times had a lot of *God, please provide* prayers. There is nothing wrong with that; we have a generous Father who loves to provide for his children. But we noticed that if we weren't careful, we could become overly focused on what we didn't have instead of giving thanks for what we did have. It was easy to look at the impending lack of finances and allow it to trouble us, get into our heads, affect our eating, and disturb our sleep. Worry sat closely at our door when we focused on what we didn't have.

The apostle Paul said, "Give thanks in all circumstances" (1 Thessalonians 5:18). In some circumstances, we gave thanks; in other circumstances, we panicked! This panic indicated that fear was sometimes getting the upper hand over trust. We realized that we would have to make a conscious effort to be thankful in all circumstances. At first, this new resolve felt a little forced, probably because it was such a planned action, but it didn't take long for it to feel natural and appropriate for our prayers to be full of thankfulness. Our primary focus became gratitude; our secondary focus became need. With our focus the right way around, we found a greater sense of quiet, calm, and stillness.

A good question we learned to ask ourselves is *Am I worrying about or being controlled by a love for money or materialism instead of trusting in God?* Thanking God for what you do have is the beginning of moving from fear to trust. We focus on what God has done and what he has given and are reminded of his provision and care for us, which builds our levels of trust.

Weirdly, even though my wife and I had less than we did before, we became more generous. Gratitude incubates generosity. A thankful and trusting heart will lead to a generous life.

Coveting

"I'm so jealous of you right now" is something I've heard often and said myself. My friends send me a photo of themselves sipping cocktails on a beach in the Maldives, and my instant reply is "I'm so jealous of you right now." Their reply is more likely to be a smiley face than "Brian, don't covet." It's a passing moment, an innocuous exchange. We all have them, and no harm is meant. But where does that start to go wrong?

"You shall not covet" is one of the Ten Commandments, given in Exodus 20:17. We don't talk much about it. We're told not to covet our neighbor's house, wife, servants, ox, donkey, or anything else that belongs to him. I'm doing quite well at not coveting anyone's ox or donkey, but I am guilty of coveting other things. I can't help wondering what would be in the list of things not to covet if it were rewritten in the twenty-first century. Some of the same things would be in there.

Interestingly, you can't really tell if someone is coveting; it is primarily an inward sin and quite easy to hide! Coveting has a lot to do with our thought lives, the starting point for breaking many of the other commandments. For example, we wouldn't steal if we hadn't first wanted something that belonged to someone else. It all begins in the head!

Coveting doesn't necessarily lead to a life of crime in which we unlawfully take what doesn't belong to us, but it can definitely get us into serious trouble. It involves desire and enticement that potentially has us fixating on a life that is different from the one we are living, wanting things we don't have and perhaps even shouldn't have. I'm fed up with living with an underlying discontent that what the Lord has provided for me isn't enough. And what happens in the head has a habit of creeping out and affecting our behavior.

Coveting is often about **MORE**. The word *more* is the opposite of the word *less*. Coveting feeds our sense of what we lack; we become fearful of having less, which will affect our ability and desire to be generous.

A mind that is always wanting more is not content.

Motivation: what drives us; why we do what we do. If our motivation is anything other than love, we will be driven to get and not to give.

Obsession: what we look at; what we spend our time on. If we are excessively fixated on something we want to have or achieve, our focus on God diminishes.

Relationships: how and why we relate to others. If our relationships are unloving and ungenerous, we will engage in favoritism or positioning ourselves to receive favor. We will fail to celebrate the blessings of others and instead wish those blessings on ourselves.

Engagement: how present we are with others and the world around us. When our minds are constantly on other things, we cease to be fully engaged and present with the people we are with—at home, with friends, at work.

If we regularly examine our approach to **MORE** through the lens of love, we will find that our living will be generous.

Contributions

A friend of mine once said, "You are best defined as a contribution, not a consumer." I am supposed to be a contribution to this planet, and that means it's more about what I give than what I get. Yet I still fall into the trap of consumerism.

Excessive consumption is encouraged by excessive promotion, which can lead to debt and a constant desire to upscale our lives. The environmental impact of easily discarded consumables is enormous—that's not being a contribution. Academics use the term *binge consuming* to describe the effects of consumerism on Western culture. In contrast, the apostle Paul talks on several occasions about pouring himself out for the sake of the gospel. This is the opposite of being a consumer. This is Paul being a contribution. He gave himself generously and fully, not pouring out just his time and money but his whole life.

I often wonder if I'm pouring myself out or just dripping a little! Generosity is about me living as a contribution in every sphere of my life: my time, my money, my service. We practice generosity and are a contribution when we listen well, speak kindly, offer our time, invite people, serve others, open our homes, give money, and share possessions. What if you asked yourself in your quiet time, *How can I be a contribution today?*

Summary

In our quiet times, we examine whether we are living generous lives, and we decide in our hearts how to cheerfully give. A little self-examination will help you identify what it looks like for you to live a generous life. Establish a habit of reviewing your generosity often.

Here are some questions to help you examine generosity in your life:

- *In what ways am I being a faithful and generous steward of God's money and possessions?*

- *Am I worrying about or being controlled by a love for money or materialism instead of trusting in God?*

- *How do I generously contribute to others with my time, my listening, my service, my words, my home, my money, and my possessions?*

- *What is my motivation—is the emphasis more on what I want to get or what I want to give? Are my desires pure?*

- *What have I been obsessing about or wanting that I don't need?*

- *Am I engaging in positioning or favoritism in my relationships in order to gain something?*

- *In what ways do I need to be more fully engaged and present in life: at home, with friends, at work?*

12

Mission and Justice

MIDAIR, POST-DINNER, settling down in my window seat for a nap, with Iran to my right and Saudi Arabia to my left, suddenly the sound of blaring alarms in the cabin shocked me into wakefulness. *Put your own mask on first.* I'd heard that sentence so many times but had never expected that I would actually need to do it.

I've heard the same words said in relation to prayer, with one bishop using them to explain that many leaders spend their time trying to help other people to put their masks on without first attending to their own. If we are trying to show other people how to inhale the deep love of the Father, we must first do so ourselves. This is true all the time and also is important to remember when it comes to mission and justice. The most fruitful people are those who have a deep and intimate relationship with God in prayer; they regularly put on their own masks first.

For more than twenty-one years, 24–7 Prayer has encouraged others to take part in an adventure of prayer, mission, and justice. At times, others have suggested, "You should just be a prayer movement or a mission movement or a justice movement—you can't be all three!" But we think the three are inseparable for Christians. Great works of justice have of course been enacted by people who are not Christians. But we never want to divorce prayer from mission or justice and lose God's power, presence, compassion, and guidance.

Breathing

In our quiet times, we breathe God in; we connect with the divine. We allow his heart to touch our hearts, and we become attuned to him. As we become aligned with God's heart and desires in quiet time, he expands our focus beyond ourselves and those most directly connected to us.

Having breathed in, we must also breathe out. Think of breathing in a natural sense—we can't just keep breathing in without also breathing out. We are healthy—actually, we are alive—when we do both! Bob Pierce, founder of World Vision, once said, "Let my heart be broken with the things that break the heart of God."[1] When we are truly connecting to the heart of God in our quiet times, he will break our hearts for his world.

Years ago, when we started praying for our work in Ibiza, I would often cry. I'm not saying that we all have to become blubbering wrecks, but God's heart will move us, and sometimes that will come out in tears. A friend who was moved by the plight of women trafficked from an African nation started to pray for them. God did something in her heart: She befriended many and went on to live and work in that nation, making a real difference in lives of returning survivors. Prayer is dangerous! As God touches our hearts, he may lead us to people or situations we could hardly have envisaged. An inevitable consequence of spending time with God, who cares about injustice and each individual, is that you will start to care, too, and your heart will be pushed to reach out to others.

Our Commission

These are the last words Matthew records Jesus saying to his disciples: "All authority in heaven and on earth has been given to me. Therefore go and make disciples of all nations, baptizing them in the name of the Father and of the Son and of the Holy Spirit, and teaching them to obey everything I have commanded you. And surely I am with you always, to the very end of the age" (Matthew 28:18-20).

The task set for the disciples was to go and make more disciples. The first thing they did after Jesus ascended to heaven was go to a secluded room and pray. The Spirit of God came powerfully, and they were propelled out of the secret room into the crowd, where they proclaimed the Good

News of Jesus. The church was born that day. It was born in prayer and fueled by the fire of the Holy Spirit. This became a continuous rhythm; they didn't pray and encounter the Holy Spirit just once; it happened again and again. The disciples and early church were caught up in the great missionary endeavor of God himself, participants in the movement of God's love toward people, with God as the fountain of that sending love.[2] When we connect with God, we experience his love, an endless, ever-flowing fountain, and we are transformed, compelled, moved, and motivated by the Holy Spirit to act on our experience.

This is our mission: that we share the love we have found. Missiologist Vincent Donovan said that the missionary is called to announce "the arrival of love on the face of the earth, love coming from the Father."[3] We announce this love because we have experienced this love in quiet time.

As you grow in your own discipleship journey, a natural overflow will be that you will seek to make more disciples, feeling that surely this love we experience is too much to be kept to ourselves. Author and theologian David J. Bosch points out that "followers of the earthly Jesus have to make others into what they themselves are: disciples."[4] This is both exciting and daunting; at times I wish I could stay in my chair, comfortably enjoying the presence of Jesus, being his disciple, learning from him. That sounds very pleasant, but it would seem that following Jesus demands a bit more!

Get Involved

Let's be clear: Prayer is prayer. It is not fuel for mission or even a strategy for mission. Yet we should learn to live with an awareness of the wider world, allowing the broken state of our world to affect us and lead us to action. Once it affects us, once we truly listen to and notice the brokenness, we seek justice. We must take Isaiah's charge to the children of Israel very seriously and apply it to our own lives:

> Learn to do right; seek justice.
>> Defend the oppressed.
> Take up the cause of the fatherless;
>> plead the case of the widow.
>
> ISAIAH 1:17

Prayer will lead us to do what is right ourselves and also to take action on behalf of others, seeking justice and defending those who are oppressed.

We learn when we listen. If we can, we should listen to the people involved in a given situation and seek to understand what the issue is. Understanding is the key to involvement in justice issues. Once we understand, we can get active. The first thing Isaiah says here is "Learn to do right." We can begin to act justly in our choices—about the food we eat, the waste we create, the way we travel, where we shop, what we wear, what we invest in, and so on. As an issue stirs us, we can sign up for newsletters so that we stay informed and know how to pray. We can give money and become regular supporters of organizations that fight the injustice. Your involvement could go further; you might volunteer with such organizations in some way or become an advocate for their work. Maybe one day, like my friend who moved to Africa, you might even train to acquire the relevant skills to make a difference on the ground and go where God leads you.

It will look different for different situations, but we can all make a noise! It can be as simple as getting people you know to sign a petition in order to lobby the government; it can be using your social media to speak out and share information to inspire others to get involved. You could speak up in your local church to raise awareness or funding, whether that be from a platform on a Sunday or a note in the church bulletin. Maybe there is a way to speak up in the wider community, too. As Micah 6:8 says,

> He has shown you, O mortal, what is good.
>   And what does the Lord require of you?
> To act justly and to love mercy
>   and to walk humbly with your God.

As well as looking at the bigger issues of injustice, we should consider the issues that affect our local areas. Find a church or community that is committed to this; most local churches will get behind someone who has a godly, prayerful passion for justice. To explore justice in your own local areas, here are three steps that will be helpful:

Explore. What is happening in your area? What are people struggling with? What are they upset about? Is there an obvious issue in your area that you can get involved with?

Educate. Know what you are doing! Research—don't run in without all the information. Some areas of injustice are complex, and some are dangerous; you need to understand what you are getting involved in.

Engage. Make a plan of how you will engage and, if you can, find other people to do it with. My advice would be not to do it alone; too many people burn out, become isolated, or place themselves in unnecessary difficulty by not working with others.

And remember: Prayer will make you an activist, but don't let your activism lead you away from prayer. You may step in in the world and try your best to effect change, but it's vital to continue to step back into prayer. Things will happen in nations around the world that we are powerless to change, but we can still pray.

Praying the News

Tragedy, danger, and death are a daily reality. News apps and websites give us ready access to what's happening in the world, and often world news events intrude into my quiet time. I believe that rather than treating these items as a nuisance, we should view them as one of the "distractions," or rather prompts, that we need to address in prayer. Here's how:

Get Informed
Gather the basics of the story from a trustworthy source. What's happening? Where? Who is affected? Who will be responding? What are the needs right now?

Pray for People
Pray for those who are negatively affected. Pray for those who have lost their families, friends, and loved ones. Pray for those who are still in danger.

Pray over Circumstances
What are the problems that only God can fix? Ask God to intervene and for God's presence to be felt.

Pray for Those in Power
Who are the decision makers who can impact the situation? Pray for mercy, compassion, and wisdom as they deal with what's happening.

Pray for the Church
Who can spread God's love and hope in the situation? Pray for pastors, churches, and nongovernmental organizations, that they would be equipped with resources, wisdom, energy, and protection for the situation.

Praying for the World

It's often the case that when we start praying about things outside our own situation or nation, the desire to do so grows and we feel the urge to pray for many other nations and people groups. Ever since I was a boy, I have been fascinated with the planet we live on. When I was a child, one of my father's friends moved to Brazil to be a missionary; each night before we went to bed, we prayed for him and the people he loved and served. As I grew older, I read stories of explorers in Africa and was fascinated by the diversity and breadth of the world that God has created. I've been able to travel to many wonderful countries around the globe; I love this planet.

There are over eight billion individuals living on our planet—people who live, act, and interact in a multiplicity of ways. This earth is diverse culturally, ethnically, religiously, and politically. At any given moment, there exist crises and pain; joy and hope; stories that lift us up and stories that bring us down. Feeling overwhelmed is one of the main challenges we face when we begin to pray for the world. Confronted with the vastness of this world and events, we think, *It's too big. There are too many problems; I can't pray for them all. Will God even hear my prayer for the world?* Here are three simple steps that I have used to help pray for the world, with its eight billion people and about 196 countries.

Step One

Start somewhere and start small. Ask God to put a country on your mind, perhaps a nation you've read about or the location of a news story that pops up in your social-media feed. Start with one nation, one that stirs your heart or catches your attention. Research your chosen country—find out about the people who live there and what the land is like. What are the challenges? What are the blessings? What's good? What's bad?

Step Two

Find out about the churches that work there and pray for them. If appropriate, get in touch with these churches and ask how you can pray.

See what mission organizations and NGOs are based there; find out their mission statements and pray into those. Think indigenously. By this, I mean look for organizations that are led by local people or are empowering local people and working in a way that is culturally sensitive.

Step Three

Commit to prayer. Pray for the leaders; pray for the economy of the land; pray for the weather; pray for the people; pray for the challenges; pray for blessing. Your quiet time will be enriched when you travel to these nations in prayer!

At a youth gathering in Germany, I met a man who had lived on the East German side of the Berlin Wall when the country was divided and Christians on that side were persecuted. He looked at me with a huge smile and said, "This is the sort of meeting I used to pray about when I was behind the wall." He may not be remembered in history as a great politician or influential world leader; he was simply a young man who prayed. Did his prayers change that part of the world? I would say that they did. Because when we learn how to pray for the world, God changes it. Your prayers could change the destiny of a nation!

Pick a Fight

I believe there should come a time when injustice in this world makes us angry. It should make us want to pick a fight. I love how Bob Goff, the author of *Love Does*, puts it: "It's easier to pick an opinion than it is to pick a fight. It's also easier to pick an organization or a jersey and identify with a fight than it is to actually go pick one, to commit to it, to call it out and take a swing. Picking a fight isn't neat either. It's messy, it's time consuming, it's painful, and it's costly. It sounds an awful lot like the kind of fight Jesus took on for us when He called out death for us and won."[5]

I have met people who have been deeply moved by certain injustices and have thrown themselves into righting those wrongs. When challenges inevitably came, some were overwhelmed; they became exhausted to the point of burnout, disillusionment, and even turning their back on their faith. Part of the problem was that they had become activists—had chosen to pick a fight—but then had allowed the demands of that activism to lead them away from regular prayer and connection with God.

The unsuccessful fighters are the ones who forget to do the training, who don't put in the hours. Muhammad Ali, arguably the greatest boxer of all time, used to go to training camps where he would spend months honing his skills and preparing for one big fight. Ali is credited with having said something along these lines: "The fight is won or lost far away from witnesses—behind the lines, in the gym, and out there on the road, long before I dance under those lights." If we plan on picking a fight with injustice, it's vital to prepare, to train ourselves so that we are spiritually healthy and fit. Your quiet time is the gym; it's the road on which you train.

What if our fights with injustice began in the gymnasium of prayer and the road of supplication—as fighters repetitively bending the knee to the will of the One who has already won in order to petition him for divine strategy, heavenly intervention, and the complete restoration and reconciliation of this broken, unjust world?

Summary
This is a small chapter about a huge subject, but I hope the points and ideas in it are helpful. Remember to breathe in and out and use these tools in your quiet time to help you engage with mission and justice. And remember, we have hope. God can—and does—change the world. Even the greatest injustice can be overcome by the power of prayer.

Ways to Pray for People Who Don't Yet Know Jesus

- Name people you would like to become Christians. Add them to your prayer list.

- Get a leather bracelet and tie knots in it to represent people you want to come to know Jesus; use this visual reminder to pray for them throughout the day.

- Place a small stone or marble in your pocket to represent a person you are praying for. Every time you sit down, you will be aware of it, which will remind you to pray.

- What other creative ways could you devise to help you pray for others?

Ways to Pray about Justice Issues

- *Use the Bible.* Write simple prayers from a particular passage (like Isaiah 58, which focuses on the issue of justice).

- *Get outside.* Go to a place connected with the issue you are praying for, such as a homeless shelter, hospital, or government building.

- *Pray with others.* Gather a group of like-minded people: Praying together is one of the best ways to keep going.

- *Be responsible.* Some issues of injustice involve crime or danger. Ensure that you don't put yourself in danger while you pray.

13

Depth

I'M NOT A NATURAL SWIMMER. I can't even tread water very well. My family members, on the other hand, swim like fish. A few years ago, we had a great opportunity to swim with a pod of wild dolphins in the Red Sea. We spent several hours on a boat heading out to where they might be; when a pod was finally spotted, we were instructed to jump off the back of the boat, which was rocking up and down in the waves, into the very deep sea in order to enjoy the spectacular sight of dolphins in the wild. My wife was the first to leap off the boat, followed by my sons. I had a split second to decide—jump now or miss this. I jumped. The depth of the water terrified me, but my fear of missing out on something special compelled me to jump. I went deeper and saw wonders!

There will come a time when your quiet time will be a beautiful and well-established part of your everyday life as a Christian. It will be life-giving, you will be growing in your faith and relationship with Jesus, and you will feel like you are in a good and secure place. At some point, you will experience a God-given desire to go deeper—God has a habit of doing that. He wants you to jump into deeper wonders, to see new things, and to experience him in new ways. He is always calling us into more until he finally calls us home to him. I like this thought! God is never finished with us; greater depth will always be something your Father wants to draw you into. Sometimes that's scary and other times it's exciting, but it's never dull! Your quiet time becomes deeper and leads to a deeper, God-centered life. This depth starts in the quiet time but ripples out into our whole lives. It leads to a holistically deeper and more connected way of life.

But what does a deeper, God-centered life really look like? When I think about going deeper, I think about the word *godliness*. As we journey deeper with the Lord, we become more godly, more like him. This is a two-way process: God works in us, and we put into place practices that enable us to move toward him. We gain a greater understanding of who God is, a more intimate experience of his love, a further understanding of his grace. Going deeper means becoming more immersed in him.

The key is to recognize that in becoming Christians, we commit to following Jesus and becoming like him. There is always more to know about God, more to learn about how to live so that we become more like him, and more to experience of him. Sometimes when I pray, I pray the simple prayer *More, Lord.* This is not the *more* of coveting that selfishly desires more things. We can cry, *More, Lord,* not because we are greedy but because God is generous.

Perhaps the desire for more of God is fueled by the desire of God himself to do more in us. After all, in Ephesians, Paul describes us as "God's handiwork," implying that God is constantly working on us—crafting, shaping, and molding us:

For it is by grace you have been saved, through
faith—and this is not from yourselves, it is the gift
of God—not by works, so that no one can boast.
For we are God's handiwork, created in Christ Jesus
to do good works, which God prepared in advance
for us to do.

EPHESIANS 2:8-10

Handiwork is translated from the Greek *poiēma*, which is the root of the word *poetry.* I like that we are God's poetry. A poem is an artistic creation, not an academic exercise; it's not functional—it is art. God is at work in us, developing our character and molding us into all he wants us to be so that we will do the good works, the godly things, that he has lined up for us. Some Greek scholars say that *poiēma* is better translated as *masterpiece.* We are God's work of art, his masterpiece. How does that sound to you? Let it sink into your soul, into your heart: You are God's masterpiece, his work of art, his poetry.

With God, we spend our lives becoming more of who we were meant to be. The learning never stops; the molding never ends. Our future is focused and positive. God is as concerned with who you are becoming as he is with who you have been. He knows your past; he is aware of your life's journey; he sees the scars you bear and the events you have experienced; he is not unaware of or uncaring about all you have suffered. But he wants to shape and mold you for the future. A friend who is an art expert explained a masterpiece to me:

> Subjectively, I would say that a masterpiece is
> like when you know you've found love. It causes
> a chemical reaction, like a physical attraction. It
> makes you wonder! A bit like a miracle, I guess. It
> surely has something to do with how much energy
> the Creator put into it. It reflects that. His passion
> becomes the viewer's passion. You know instantly
> when you encounter a masterpiece.

God is dedicated to continue the masterful work he began in you until it is complete. Paul confidently tells us, "I am sure of this, that he who began a good work in you will bring it to completion at the day of Jesus Christ" (Philippians 1:6, ESV).

Sometimes going deeper will be fostered by circumstances. Other times, it will be because you have made a conscious decision to go deeper. Inside and outside our quiet times, there are intentional actions we can take as we seek to go deeper with God. We grow in godliness as we find our identity in the quiet time. As we desire more of him, we want to go deeper, and there are some real, practical steps we can take to help us.

Study Will Take You Deeper

Our faith isn't purely cerebral and only for academics, but there is real depth to gain from study. Study could involve listening to podcasts; there are some great thinkers constantly shedding light and offering insight on Scripture. A church leader or trusted friend might be able to make some recommendations.

A study Bible is also helpful; these give a little more information on the text at the bottom of each page that helps in understanding context and history and some of the thinking behind what you are reading.

Theologians and Bible teachers have written books that are companions for specific books of the Bible. I personally enjoy The Bible Speaks Today commentary series, which offers a scholarly look at each book of the Bible along with theological insight and historical illumination in a very accessible format. There are lots of other books: commentaries ranging from the thick and weighty to the more easily readable; books that explain certain doctrines and stances on the various elements of our faith; books about church history and how we got where we are today.

Remember, the purpose of study isn't solely to acquire

knowledge; the purpose is to go deeper. Have a reread of the chapter on Scripture in this book. As you study, have the same approach as you have for your quiet time, studying from a place of stillness with a quiet spirit and a learning heart and continuing to pray, *Speak, Lord, for your servant is listening.*

Serving Will Take You Deeper

Serving is foot washing! John 13 records the beautiful story of Jesus washing his disciples' feet. In those days, most people walked to get around; the paths were dusty, and the climate was mostly dry and hot. Feet became grimy. In a household that had servants, one of them would be given the task of washing the feet of guests. It certainly would not have been the task carried out by the most important person present, the master.

But on this occasion, Jesus took up the water and towels and started to wash the feet of his disciples. This was the wrong way around! The disciples recognized this instantly and felt awkward and uncomfortable—so much so that one of them blurted out, "No way! You're not washing my feet" (PAR). But Jesus continued. With the task completed, he sat down and asked his disciples,

> Do you understand what I have done to you? You call me Teacher and Lord, and you are right, for so I am. If I then, your Lord and Teacher, have washed your feet, you also ought to wash one another's

feet. For I have given you an example, that you also should do just as I have done to you.

JOHN 13:12-15, ESV

This is an instruction for us, too. We are called to live life as servants, a life of servanthood. A servant serves when no one is watching. A servant never asks, "What's in it for me?" It's worth once more thinking about generosity when it comes to serving: How can we be generous servants?

We should regularly look for ways we can serve. Whether it's volunteering in your local church or with a charity, helping out at a kids' club, or giving up your evenings to teach immigrants English, there are many ways to serve locally that will only cost your time. Serve locally before you think of serving globally. As we serve, we grow closer to Jesus, who served. It becomes part of the way we live.

Serving on a Mission Team Will Take You Deeper

As a church youth worker many years ago, I took teams of young people to help with a homeless project in New York. The work was physically demanding; it was intensely hot and humid; it was emotionally challenging to see people in various states of distress. But we served. And we learned so much, from serving itself and also from the shared experience of working closely and under pressure doing something we felt Jesus would have done. When we are out of our comfort zones and normal environments, we learn a lot about God, about others, and about ourselves.

Mission teams are also a wonderful way to enlarge our thoughts in regard to mission and justice. As the years went by, I became a bit concerned that some mission teams appeared to be a little like Christian tourist groups—affluent Western Christians ambling up to an orphanage of abandoned children in Kenya, bringing fun, laughter, gifts, and lots of attention for two weeks and then going home and abandoning them! Instead, I encourage you to find a mission team that serves a community, one that is more about development than support. Make sure it's one that aims to bolster and serve the local people in a way that is genuinely constructive. When we led the work of 24–7 Prayer in Ibiza, we couldn't have achieved all that we were building every summer without the help of mission teams, but it's important to remember that mission teams should be all about the people you're serving, not you.

Retreats Will Take You Deeper
Employment contracts of every employee of 24–7 Prayer require them to take one day each month for retreat. The working day is given to prayer and reflection because we see the necessity of retreat in going deeper with God. The plan for the retreat day is not prescribed and could include things like reading, going for a long walk, visiting a church, journaling—anything that dedicates time and thought to God. Your employment contract may not give you this opportunity, but I would still encourage you to find a way to retreat that suits your character and the ways of reflecting

that you find most constructive. I have been on silent retreats; for some people, this is the absolute ideal, but personally, I find it to be a struggle! I have also gone away for twenty-four hours to pray, reflect, and gather my thoughts. Another option is to go on a guided retreat, where you can be led through various activities or spiritual practices. These are often led by individuals or written guides that help shape the retreat time.

When we retreat, we retreat from work, retreat from our usual rhythms, retreat from busyness, and retreat from people in order to spend a prolonged quiet time with the Lord. Journeys into hiddenness often begin on retreats.

Pilgrimages Will Take You Deeper

Some people go on journeys to ancient sites in order to get a feel for things that happened there in the past: old revival spots, places where people were martyred, sites where miracles took place or visions were seen. Visits like these can spark your imagination and stir your faith as they connect you to the bigger story of faith through history.

Other people go to churches where God seems to be doing extraordinary things in order to experience firsthand what is happening. My personal pilgrimages are often to churches in traditions that I am not currently part of; I have experienced fresh insight, understanding, and depth in things that are different from what is traditional for me. Although I was brought up in a Protestant church and still practice my faith within that tradition, my life has been greatly enriched by the Catholic Church and the warmth and authenticity of the people I have met in it. I have learned a lot from Catholic devotion and the richness of Catholic tradition.

The Depth of Crisis

Sometimes what takes us deeper is not something we choose or even want; it's not always something that we make happen but sometimes something that happens to us. I have friends who have been through incredible times of pain, sorrow, and loss; they didn't ask for them, they didn't deserve them, they didn't bring them upon themselves, and they would rather not have suffered them. Yet they have emerged from those dark times as deeper, more godly people. God has a way of bringing beautiful things out of even the most difficult, ugly times.

A friend and I went through a particularly difficult time in which we felt really let down by a senior leader. We were disappointed and disillusioned because someone we loved and admired had made a serious mistake and ultimately made some choices that were incompatible with staying in his leadership role. I was devastated; he was my hero. I'd wanted to be like him, but he let me down. My friend and I phoned each other often as we processed our shared disappointment. One night when I asked how he was doing, he replied, "Sometimes I sit on the end of my bed and think, *Is this all worth it?* And then I choose to believe. Sometimes, Brian, we just have to choose to believe even if we don't feel like it." The crisis took him deeper. He didn't want it; he didn't ask for it; but when it came, he chose to believe despite the crisis.

It's often not in the midst of the crisis but *after* we have been in the crisis for a while that we experience the sense of going deeper. My friend is a deeper man today because of the way he faced that time.

Delicate Refinement

Charles Spurgeon once said, "All that a college course can do for a student is coarse and external compared with the spiritual and delicate refinement obtained by communion with God."[1] I love that phrase: *delicate refinement*. It's so gentle. God delicately refines you into the masterpiece he longs for you to be. God is always gentle, always kind, even when the circumstances are tough. When we face areas of sin or are confronted with unhealthy patterns of behavior that we need to let go of, he is kind.

Psalm 23 is arguably the most famous psalm and talks about God as the Shepherd, saying, "He makes me lie down in green pastures" (Psalm 23:2). Bible commentator Rolf Jacobson says that this translation is a bit wooden and doesn't fully convey the love of God as the Shepherd; he says that the phrase *he makes me* "denotes the active agency of the shepherd in seeking out an environment in which the sheep may thrive."[2] God is delicately refining us; he is constantly seeking to lead us into an environment where we will thrive.

Summary

Going deeper is important. We can embrace this journey into godliness, allowing it to permeate every part of our lives, from the quiet time and beyond. Therefore, while being refined by what happens on your journey in order that you can thrive, here are some questions you may find helpful:

- How does it feel to be described as God's masterpiece, his poetry, his work of art?

- How can you serve locally? In your church? In your community? In your family? Among your friends or colleagues?

- If you could go overseas with a mission team, where would you go and why?

- Where would you be interested in visiting as a pilgrimage? How can you make that happen?

Here are some helpful exercises:

- Pick one book of the Bible and study it. Find out when it was written, who it was originally addressed to, and how it has been received by others over the years. What is contentious within it? What is reassuring?

- Go deep into one entire book of the Bible. Remember to enter with a prayer of *Speak, Lord, for your servant is listening.*

- Take a day off and use it as a retreat day. Go for a walk, reflect on Scripture, read a book, look at some art. Try giving eight hours of the day to this.

- Arrange to go to another church one week; attend a church service that is different from one in your own tradition. What do you notice? What is different? What does this church have in common with yours? What does the different style add to your current understanding?

14

Seasons

THE PSALMIST SAYS, "Taste and see that the LORD is good"
(Psalm 34:8). The prophet/poet Isaiah says,

> "Come, all you who are thirsty,
> come to the waters;
> and you who have no money,
> come, buy and eat!
> Come, buy wine and milk
> without money and without cost.
> Why spend money on what is not bread,
> and your labor on what does not satisfy?
> Listen, listen to me, and eat what is good,
> and you will delight in the richest of fare."

ISAIAH 55:1-2

In my Bible, the heading reads, "An Invitation to the Thirsty." I would lengthen this to "An Invitation to the Thirsty and the Hungry." We have a beautiful banquet set before us, a real delight, an opportunity to taste and see that the Lord is good. The table is loaded with the richest of fare. The beckoning call of God to each one of us is this invitation to the thirsty and the hungry: "Come eat, come taste, come experience all that I have for you." There will be different meals in different seasons of your life, different dishes that you will taste as you sit with God in your quiet time. As you thirstily and hungrily pursue encounters with God, each season of your life will be filled with the richest of fare. My invitation is that you draw up a chair, or take a walk in the garden, and feast on all that he has for you.

This feast can be experienced in the breaking light of the morning, on your commute, in a sweaty gym, on your lunch break, or in the cool of the day. You can find God in your chair, on your dog walk, under the shade of a tree, or even under your duvet. This feeling, this connection, this kind of encounter, can take place in a prison, a palace, a church sanctuary, a garden, or your car—anywhere you are, he is. The quiet time is the prayerful place of encounter. The chair we sit in and the garden we walk in will become a beautiful constant in our lives, even though our lives are always changing. Our quiet times will look different depending on what spiritual season we find ourselves in.

In the quiet time, you can grow in your understanding of the Bible, hiding the Word of God in your heart as you memorize and meditate on it. In the quiet time, you will learn to examine your life. It's a time to exercise the practice of journaling, to consider what it means to live simply, stop to wonder, and engage your imagination. The quiet time will lead you to other challenges—into walking a path of perseverance and establishing a habit of fasting. You will grow in your understanding of living counterculturally: seeking hiddenness in an age of promotion, embracing generosity instead of selfishness, expressing gratitude instead of coveting, and being a contribution rather than a consumer. As you align your heart with God's heart, your love for people and for justice will expand, propelling you toward servanthood, mission, and the pursuit of justice. As you go deeper in your quiet time, you will grow in godliness and embrace what you learn through tough times. This doesn't happen overnight but grows in us as we journey through the *seasons* of life.

Notice the Seasons

One of the few benefits of the COVID-19 pandemic of 2020–2021 for me—when we were all instructed to stay local and exercise was confined to one walk per day—was observing the seasons. I live in a rural part of England, where agriculture is one of the main industries, but I had never taken the time to stop and notice the seasons that were necessary for growth and the production of crops. My focus had been much narrower, thinking mostly about the impact the weather had on my plans and personal enjoyment. Now I have passed the same fields through the changing seasons of the year; I have seen them fallow and full, green and golden. Each stage is necessary in its own way to allow for the seed to be planted, take root, shoot, and grow into all that it is meant to be. I have four prints hanging on my bedroom wall of a beautiful series of paintings by the Spanish artist Eusebio Sempere called *Las Cuatro Estaciones*, which represent the four seasons. They are very simple yet somehow convey the different tones, hues, and colors of the seasons.

Different seasons provide different experiences, and we approach each of them differently; in the natural world, different food is available, different amounts of light, different temperatures. We can look at the seasons of life spiritually as well as naturally, and our quiet times will be affected and molded by the seasons of life. Ecclesiastes 3:1 tells us, "There is a time for everything, and a season for every activity under the heavens." The seasons are interdependent and interconnected; every season sees the departure of one creature and arrival of another. The seasons can also be a mirror to the spirituality of our own lives, and each season has different dishes on which to feast.

Spring is a season of new life, birth, and beginning. When you find yourself in a spring season with your quiet time, you will feel full of life. You can be engaged in new ventures and approach your time with God with fresh excitement. The world seems full of possibilities—there will be fervor, excitement, and energy in your times with God.

This is the time to strengthen your heart, memorize and meditate on the Word, and feed your soul.

Summer is a time of harvest, fruitfulness, and productivity. When you find yourself in a summer season, you might find that you want to focus on the work at hand. You're in a time of results and high function, and it's here that the temptation will come to shorten your time with God, to crack on with the day. It's very important in this season to stop and look up. Don't let what you are doing obscure the One you are doing it for! Look up, look back, look forward—most importantly, make time to wonder.

Autumn is a time of change, beauty, and preparation. Finding yourself in an autumnal season, your quiet time will be full of gratitude, mirroring the harvest festivals held to give thanks for all the good that the Lord has done. Gratitude is often a reflective process that leads to a season of evaluation. Seasons with an autumn feel can be times to check what you are treasuring and examine what you might need to give up: Could a time of fasting or abstinence help you? The slowing of pace will also give you the space to check your anxiety.

Winter is a time of rest, pruning, and dying. Finding yourself in a time of winter can be the sweetest of experiences; you will find time to rest, to sit in the chair and kick back. In such times, you will feel the warmth and the closeness of the Father. You may think of winter as a time that feels harsh, barren, and lacking in life, but a lot takes place in the hiddenness of it. You grow in perseverance in winter. You may have to cling on a little bit and work not to give up, but the joy in holding on is strengthened by the knowledge that after every winter there is a spring.

Seasons are necessary; they allow for death, regrowth, rebirth, rest, restoration, growth, incubation, and so much more, very often blending and merging. They each serve a specific function; the implicitly wonderful thing about seasons, especially the tough ones, is that they pass.

Apart from seasons that mirror the natural world, we also experience seasons that are more like stages of life, and our quiet times will look different throughout those as well.

Waiting Seasons (You Will Have to Wait)
There will be seasons when you will be asked to wait, when you will want to move on but will feel constrained by time and circumstances. There is a lot to be learned in a season of waiting, but two things I really think will help are *Be patient* and *Be present*.

When I read back through my journal entries written in seasons of waiting, it's clear that my impatience for what is next has often made it hard for me to be fully present. C. S. Lewis writes of the danger of only ever being focused on the past or the future, saying that "the Future is . . . the most completely temporal part of time—for the Past is frozen and no longer flows, and the Present is all lit up with eternal rays."[1]

In a season of waiting, don't remain in a place of regret, saying, *If only* or *I wish* as you look back; meanwhile, don't allow looking forward to dominate your thoughts so that they're all about "one day." Let's be clear: I am not encouraging the "live in the moment" attitude of hedonism. It is good to reflect on the past and plan for the future—but not if it's fueled by impatience, frustration, or nostalgia for a moment that has gone or is still yet to be. Live in the present, which is "all lit up with eternal rays"; the here and now is important to you and who you are in this season.

Dying Seasons (There Will Be Death)

As a Christian, my faith is built on the reality of Christ's death and resurrection; however, I am still not entirely comfortable with seasons of death. A friend was nursing his father in his final days; although he was a Christian, his father became a bit scared and nervous toward the end. My friend gently and kindly said to his father, "It takes as much faith to die as it does to live." I think that also applies when the death we are facing is not a literal passing away. Do we have the faith to allow things to die, to let things go, to move on, to finish something, to walk away? This is one of the most demanding kinds of season you will ever experience: a season of the death of something that has been important to you. Jesus said, "Unless a kernel of wheat falls to the ground and dies, it remains only a single seed. But if it dies, it produces many seeds" (John 12:24).

What are you being asked to let die right now? Is it a relationship, a position, a job, a dream, an organization, a ministry? Our faith is built around the centrality of death and resurrection, yet often we seem to struggle with death. Perhaps this isn't the best way to put it and sounds overly dark and dramatic, but *embrace death*. Think about words like *stop*, *change*, *move*, and *leave*; it's good to recognize these words as markers of putting something down, of letting go. Death, letting go, is never easy and sometimes unanticipated, but it's often necessary for something new to be born.

Changing Seasons (Change Is Constant)

Change is inevitable. There are changes that we can prevent, resist, or slow down, but since everything doesn't depend on us, change will come in some form. Some people like change, or at least what change seems to promise. Others prefer the comfort of familiarity and things remaining the same. Some changes will bring joy, hope, and excitement. Other changes will cause us to feel uncertain, insecure, and fearful. Yet change is certain—it will come.

Anchored Seasons (You Will Have to Make Sacrifices)

Anchors can be responsibilities, obligations, and commitments that we have made. Elderly parents, children at key stages in the educational system, health challenges, job contracts, and financial constraints can all be anchors. Anchors hold us in place, stop us from drifting, prevent us from moving on. They keep us fixed to a place.

Fulfilling the responsibilities that come with an anchor will often mean that we have to sacrifice other things, things we would have really liked to do. Don't blame the anchor or become frustrated with it; find joy and accept the anchor as appropriate for the season. Embrace the sacrifice—there is an understanding of God's sacrificial nature to be gained. Ask yourself what your obligations and responsibilities are teaching you.

The Surprise of Stillness

There have been very clear and definite seasons in my life. Some have been fulfilling, some have been challenging, and some have even been dark! There have been seasons when my quiet times have felt fresh and energized; there have been other seasons when I have barely been able to muster any enthusiasm. I have had quiet times that have lasted three minutes and lived through other days without really turning to my Father for any meaningful time whatsoever. I'm reassured that God understands when we fragile beings on occasion exhibit our fragility.

I'm still surprised by God. He is bursting with new things—his creativity and ways of engaging with me appear to know no bounds. He draws me into the quiet time and regularly puts new dishes before me to taste. I'm amazed at his generosity. Time and time again, he meets us—his flawed, weak, distracted creations—with unrivaled generosity, love, and kindness.

As I regularly approach my quiet time, I am reassured that I am approaching a loving and wild yet stable God; he is full of surprises but going nowhere! He waits for me, he draws me deeper, he calls me to adventure. Over the years, it's been clear that whatever season I am going through, he is there. Not once has he let me down; he has been faithful, constant, and true. My prayer is that you, too, will journey through the seasons of life with a quiet time that feeds you. So find your chair, grab your coffee, and settle in for an adventurous life of quiet stillness.

Let me leave you with a blessing—my prayer—for your quiet time.

May your chair be blessed with the presence of the divine.
May your walk with God be a pleasure that sustains you.
Let his Word feed you, his world speak to you, and his
Spirit fuel your imagination.
Write of his goodness, speak of his kindness, practice
gratitude, always trust.
May your more be only for him and your less only to sin.
Stop, look up, and wonder at all you see.
Live simply.
Find God in hiddenness and hide him in you. Have the
tenacity of perseverance; fight!
Find joy in giving; pour yourself out; live your life for
others.

*Carry Christ's love to the lost, his freedom to captives, his
comfort to the broken, and his healing to the sick.
Get lost in the depths of the Father's love; find yourself in
him.
Enjoy the feast; embrace the seasons.
Be still and know that he is God.
Amen.*

Acknowledgments

TRACY, THIS BOOK WOULD NEVER have happened without you. Thank you for putting up with my dodgy grammar and asking me the hard questions that made my writing better—you are my sunshine. To Daniel, Ellis, and Natasha: This book is for you guys. You bring the joy and provide the inspiration as you work out your lives of faith in such authentic ways.

Mike Andrea, your friendship, leadership, and support have been exemplary—thank you. Pete Greig, your helpful insights and constant encouragement always help me in those moments of self-doubt. Joanna Callender, without your eye for detail and ability to see what would read well, this would have been a car crash.

To the 24–7 Prayer team, especially the early-morning check-in posse, these last eighteen months have been strange and joyful. Without you guys being there every morning, it would have been nearly impossible; so thank you, Carla, Nick, Richard, Rich, Ebony, Emily, Holly, Tandia, Jake, Wardy, Rachel, Roger, Jill, Phil, Ian, Laura, Tanya, and Keith.

Hannah Heather, thank you so much for originally inviting me to speak with students and inspiring me to take this further. And to Charles and Margaret Douglas: Your prayerful support has been so helpful throughout this entire process; thank you.

Huge thanks, of course, to Elizabeth Neep and the team at SPCK; thank you for your patience and encouragement.

Bibliography

Barclay, William. *The Gospel of Matthew: Volume 1*. Edinburgh, UK: Saint Andrew Press, 2009.

Beckett, Sister Wendy. *The Story of Painting*. London: DK, 2000.

Bosch, David J. *Transforming Mission*. Maryknoll, NY: Orbis, 2011.

Chesterton, G. K. *Orthodoxy*. New York: Shaw, 2001.

Comer, John Mark. *The Ruthless Elimination of Hurry*. London: Hodder & Stoughton, 2019.

Crossway (website). "Infographic: You Have More Time for Bible Reading than You Think," November 19, 2018, https://www.crossway.org>articles /infographic-you-can-read-more-of-the-bible-than-you-think.

Donovan, Vincent J. *Christianity Rediscovered*. 4th ed. London. SCM, 2009.

Dostoevsky, Fyodor. *The Brothers Karamazov*. New York: Macmillan, 1912.

Ellicott, C. J. *A Bible Commentary for English Readers*, vol. 1, London: Cassell, 1884.

Emerson, Alain. *Luminous Dark*. Edinburgh, UK: Muddy Pearl, 2017.

Foster, Richard J. *Celebration of Discipline*. London: Hodder & Stoughton, 2008.

France, R. T. *The Gospel of Matthew*. Grand Rapids, MI: Wm. B. Eerdmans, 2007.

Gabel, Helmut. "Ignatian Contemplation and Modern Biblical Studies." *The Way* 44, no. 2 (2005).

Goff, Bob. *Love Does: Discover a Secretly Incredible Life in an Ordinary World*. Edinburgh, UK: Thomas Nelson, 2012.

Goldingay, John. *An Ignatian Approach to Reading the Old Testament*. Cambridge, UK: Grove, 2002.

Graham-Dixon, Andrew. *Caravaggio: A Life Sacred and Profane*. London: Penguin, 2011.

Greig, Pete. *God on Mute: Engaging the Silence of Unanswered Prayer*. Chester, UK: Kingsway, 2007.

———. *How to Pray: A Simple Guide for Normal People*. London: Hodder & Stoughton, 2019.

Keller, Tim. *Generous Justice: How God's Grace Makes Us Just*. London: Hodder & Stoughton, 2010.

Kidner, Derek. "Genesis 2:5, 6: Wet or Dry?" *Tyndale Bulletin* 17 (1966).

Kierkegaard, Søren. *For Self-Examination / Judge for Yourself!: Kierkegaard's Writings, XXI, Volume 21*, ed. and trans. Howard V. Hong and Edna H. Hong. Princeton, NJ: Princeton University Press, 1991.

Klinger, Eric. *Daydreaming: Using Waking Fantasy and Imagery for Self-Knowledge and Creativity*. Los Angeles: Jeremy P. Tarcher, 1990.

Leonhardt, Douglas J. *Finding God in All Things*. Milwaukee: Marquette University Press, 2009.

Lewis, C. S. *The Screwtape Letters*. London: Fount Paperbacks, 1977.

———. *The Weight of Glory and Other Addresses*. New York: HarperCollins, 2013.

Martin, James. *The Jesuit Guide to (Almost) Everything*. New York: Orbis, 2012.

McKnight, Scot. *Fasting*. Edinburgh, UK: Thomas Nelson, 2010.

Motyer, J. Alec. *The Prophecy of Isaiah: An Introduction Commentary*. Downers Grove, IL: InterVarsity Press, 1998.

Oatman, Johnson, Jr. "Count Your Blessings." Hymn.

Peterson, Eugene. *Eat This Book*. London: John Murray, 2008.

Portal, Pete. *No Neutral Ground*. London: Hodder & Stoughton, 2019.

The Simpsons, season 2, episode 4, "Two Cars in Every Garage and Three Eyes on Every Fish."

Sparrow, Betsy, Jenny Liu, and Daniel M. Wehner. "Google Effects on Memory: Cognitive Consequences of Having Information at Our Fingertips," *Science* 333 (2011).

Strong, James. *The New Strong's Expanded Exhaustive Concordance of the Bible*. Edinburgh, UK: Thomas Nelson, 2010.

Valerio, Ruth. *Saying Yes to Life*. London: SPCK, 2019.

———. *L Is for Lifestyle*. London: IVP, 2019.

Wallis, Arthur. *God's Chosen Fast*. Fort Washington, PA: CLC, 2015.

Ware, Bishop Kallistos. *The Jesus Prayer*. London: Catholic Truth Society, 2014.

White, Aaron. *Recovering: From Brokenness and Addiction to Blessedness and Community*. Pastoring for Life: Theological Wisdom for Ministering Well. Grand Rapids, MI: Baker Academic, 2020.

Willard, Dallas. *The Spirit of the Disciplines*. San Francisco: Harper, 1990.

Wordsworth, William. *The Prelude, or Growth of a Poet's Mind*. Boston: D.C. Heath, 1888.

Notes

FOREWORD
1. Henri J. M. Nouwen, *The Way of the Heart: Desert Spirituality and Contemporary Ministry* (San Fransisco: HarperSanFransisco, 1991), 30.

CHAPTER 1 | ENCOUNTER
1. *A Bible Commentary for English Readers*, ed. Charles J. Ellicott, vol. 1, *Genesis–Esther* (Harrington, DE: Delmarva, 2015), Genesis 3:8.

CHAPTER 2 | DISTRACTION
1. *Cambridge Dictionary*, s.v. "distraction (*n.*)," accessed October 18, 2022, https://dictionary.cambridge.org/us/dictionary/english/distraction.
2. R. T. France, *Matthew: An Introduction and Commentary*, Tyndale New Testament Commentaries (Downers Grove, IL: IVP Academic, 2015), 137.
3. "If I were a physician, and if I were allowed to prescribe just one remedy for all the ills of the modern world, I would prescribe silence. For even if the Word of God were proclaimed in the modern world, how could one hear it with so much noise? Therefore, create silence." Søren Kierkegaard, *For Self-Examination / Judge for Yourself!: Kierkegaard's Writings, XXI, Volume 21* (Princeton, NJ: Princeton University Press, 1991).
4. Eric Klinger, *Daydreaming: Using Waking Fantasy and Imagery for Self-Knowledge and Creativity* (Los Angeles: Jeremy P. Tarcher, 1990), xi.
5. C. S. Lewis, *The Weight of Glory and Other Addresses* (New York: HarperCollins, 2001), 60.
6. Bishop Kallistos Ware, *The Jesus Prayer* (London: Catholic Truth Society, 2014), "The Four Strands."

CHAPTER 3 | SCRIPTURE
1. Quoted, for example, by Pope Francis. See "Pope Quotes Gandhi to Encourage Bible Reading," *Matters India*, February 28, 2016, https://mattersindia.com/2016/02/pope-quotes-gandhi-to-encourage-bible-reading.
2. *Merriam-Webster*, s.v. "religious (*adj.*)," accessed October 18, 2022, https://www.merriam-webster.com/dictionary/religious.
3. Charles H. Spurgeon, *Lectures to My Students: A Selection from Addresses Delivered to the Students of the Pastors' College, Metropolitan Tabernacle* (New York: Sheldon & Company, 1875), 69.
4. Crossway, "Infographic: You Have More Time for Bible Reading than You Think," November 19, 2018, https://www.crossway.org/articles/infographic-you-can-read-more-of-the-bible-than-you-think.
5. "Average Daily Time Spent on Social Media (Latest 2022 Data)," Broadband Search.net, accessed October 17, 2022, https://www.broadbandsearch.net/blog/average-daily-time-on-social-media.
6. This quote seems to have originated with Confucius, though I encountered it from Andy Warhol.

CHAPTER 4 | MEMORIZE AND MEDITATE
1. Betsy Sparrow, Jenny Liu, and Daniel M. Wegner, "Google Effects on Memory: Cognitive Consequences of Having Information at Our Fingertips," *Science* 333, no. 6043 (2011): 776–8.
2. Gleason Archer, *Greekmaster with Gleason Archer* (Battle Ground, WA: The Gramcord Institute), CD-ROM.
3. James Strong, *The New Strong's Expanded Exhaustive Concordance of the Bible* (Edinburgh, UK: Thomas Nelson, 2010).
4. "Psalm 1: The Way of Life," in Nancy Declaissé-Walford, Rolf A. Jacobson, and Beth Laneel Tanner, *The Book of Psalms*, New International Commentary on the Old Testament (Grand Rapids, MI: Eerdmans, 2014), 61.

CHAPTER 5 | JOURNALING
1. Delirious? "Obsession," *Cutting Edge* © 1998 Sparrow Records.
2. William Wordsworth, *The Prelude or Growth of a Poet's Mind* (Boston: D. C. Heath, 1888).
3. Johnson Oatman Jr., "Count Your Blessings," 1897. Public domain.

CHAPTER 6 | IMAGINATION
1. N. T. Wright, "Jesus, the Cross and the Power of God" (conference paper, European Leaders' Conference, Warsaw, Poland, 2006).

2. Sister Wendy Beckett, *The Story of Painting* (London: Dorling Kindersley, 1994), 318.
3. Andrew Graham-Dixon, *Caravaggio: A Life Sacred and Profane* (London: Penguin, 2011), 31.
4. John Goldingay, *An Ignatian Approach to Reading the Old Testament* (Cambridge, UK: Grove Books, 2002).
5. Douglas J. Leonhardt, *Finding God in All Things* (Milwaukee: Marquette University Press, 2009), as quoted here: https://www.ignatianspirituality.com/ignatian-prayer/the-what-how-why-of-prayer/praying-with-scripture/page (accessed September 15, 2021).
6. Helmut Gabel, "Ignatian Contemplation and Modern Biblical Studies," *The Way* 44, no. 2 (2005): 37–49.

CHAPTER 7 | WONDER
1. Mary Oliver, "Upstream" in *Upstream: Selected Essays* (New York: Penguin Books, 2019), 8.
2. Derek Kidner, *Genesis*, Tyndale Old Testament Commentaries, vol. 1 (Downers Grove, IL: IVP Academic, 2008), Genesis 28:10-22.
3. Fyodor Dostoevsky, *The Brothers Karamazov*, bicentennial ed., trans. Richard Pevear and Larissa Volokhonsky (New York: Picador, 2021), 384.
4. Keith Fournier, "The End of the Year: A Christian Reflection on Time," Catholic Online, January 2, 2015, https://www.catholic.org/news/hf/faith/story.php?id=53724.
5. Graham Kendrick, *Worship* (London: Kingsway Publications, 1984).
6. Francis Chan with Danae Yankoski, *Crazy Love: Overwhelmed by a Relentless God* (Colorado Springs, CO: David C Cook, 2013), 33.
7. G. K. Chesterton, *Orthodoxy* (New York: John Lane Co., 1908), 108–109.

CHAPTER 8 | PERSEVERING
1. J. Alec Motyer, *The Message of Exodus: The Days of Our Pilgrimage*, rev. ed., The Bible Speaks Today (Downers Grove, IL: IVP Academic, 2021), 172.
2. Albert Barnes, *Notes, Critical, Explanatory, and Practical, on the Book of the Prophet Isaiah*, vol. II, 2nd ed. (New York: Leavitt, Trow and Co., 1847), 394.

CHAPTER 9 | SIMPLICITY
1. Richard J. Foster, *Celebration of Discipline: The Path to Spiritual Growth*, special anniv. ed. (New York: HarperSanFrancisco, 1998), 79.
2. Dallas Willard, *The Spirit of the Disciplines: Understanding How God Changes Lives* (New York: HarperCollins, 1991), 166.

3. John Wesley, *Sermons on Several Occasions*, vol. I (London: Wesleyan Conference Office, 1864), 336.
4. As quoted in Dallas Willard, *The Spirit of the Disciplines*, 167.

CHAPTER 10 | HIDDEN LIFE
1. William Barclay, *The Gospel of John*, vol. 1, The New Daily Study Bible (Louisville, KY: Westminster John Knox Press, 2017), 270.

CHAPTER 11 | GENEROSITY
1. Timothy Keller, *Generous Justice: How God's Grace Makes Us Just* (New York: Riverhead Books, 2012), 91.
2. Dictionary.com, s.v. "steward (*n.*)," accessed October 20, 2022, https://www.dictionary.com/browse/steward.
3. "Two Cars in Every Garage and Three Eyes on Every Fish," *The Simpsons*, season 2, episode 4.

CHAPTER 12 | MISSION AND JUSTICE
1. Bob Pierce, quoted in Rich Stearns, "Blessed by a Broken Heart," *Voices* (blog), World Vision, August 28, 2017, https://www.worldvision.org/hunger-news-stories/blessed-broken-heart.
2. David J. Bosch, *Transforming Mission: Paradigm Shifts in Theology of Mission*, 8th ed. (Maryknoll, NY: Orbis Books, 1995), 400.
3. Vincent J. Donovan, *Christianity Rediscovered*, 4th ed. (London: SCM Press, 2009), 141.
4. David J. Bosch, *Transforming Mission*, 75.
5. Bob Goff, *Love Does: Discover a Secretly Incredible Life in an Ordinary World* (Nashville, TN: Thomas Nelson, 2012), 196.

CHAPTER 13 | DEPTH
1. Charles H. Spurgeon, *Lectures to My Students: A Selection from Addresses Delivered to the Students of the Pastors' College, Metropolitan Tabernacle* (New York: Sheldon & Company, 1875), 68.
2. "Psalm 23: You Are with Me," in Nancy L. deClaissé-Walford, Rolf A. Jacobson, and Beth LaNeel Tanner, *The Book of Psalms*, The New International Commentary on the Old Testament (Grand Rapids, MI: Eerdmans, 2014), 241.

CHAPTER 14 | SEASONS
1. C. S. Lewis, *The Screwtape Letters* (New York: HarperOne, 2001), 76.

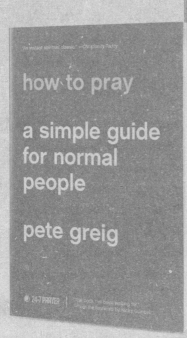